D0852469

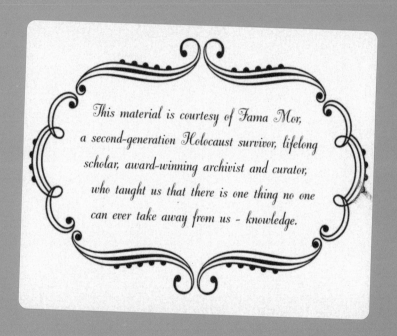

The Story of
the Synagogue

The Story of
THE SYNAGOGUE

A Diaspora Museum Book

Geoffrey Wigoder

The Domino Press
Jerusalem

Chief Editor: Uri Ram
Photo Researcher: Tamar Manor

The Domino Press
38 Hatayasim Street, Jerusalem

By arrangement with
George Weidenfeld and Nicolson Limited
91 Clapham High Street, London SW4 7TA

Colour Separations by Newsele Litho Ltd
Filmset by Keyspools Ltd, Golborne, Lancs
Printed and bound by L.E.G.O., Vicenza, Italy

CONTENTS

FOREWORD   7

The Beginnings   9

The Classical Period   17

Medieval Europe   35

Spain and Portugal   57

Renaissance and Ghetto   73

Eastern Europe   93

Towards Emancipation   113

In Moslem Lands   131

Far-Off Places   149

Equal Citizens   167

Meeting Modern Challenges   185

GLOSSARY   203

INDEX   205

FOREWORD

THE uninterrupted existence of the Jewish people down the ages raises the question which Beth Hatefutsoth, Tel Aviv's Diaspora Museum, attempts to answer: how is it that, despite such adverse circumstances as recurring persecution, discrimination, pogroms, and, eventually, the Holocaust, the Jews, scattered to all four corners of the world, continued their corporate existence in creativity and dignity? The Museum suggests that the answer lies in the six pillars of Jewish existence: the family, the community, the Jewish faith, education and culture, peoplehood, and the longing for Zion.

The Jewish faith has always had two major focuses for observance and expression: the family circle and the synagogue, the heart of ritual and prayer which began with the Temple in Jerusalem and developed into the multitude of prayer-houses created by Jews wherever they lived. The synagogue is surely one of Judaism's greatest inspirations to mankind, for it engendered, in turn, the church and the mosque. It is the synagogue, illustrated through a series of models portraying its development through time and place, that is the core of the Diaspora Museum's 'Faith' section. And it is the story of the synagogue that is told in these pages, with many of its illustrations drawn from the meticulously accurate models of that Museum. These models were carefully selected to reflect different styles and periods, from the third to the twentieth century, as well as many parts of the world. Eighteen synagogues are reproduced as models and four in environmental fragments (Dura-Europos, Syria; El Transito, Toledo, Spain; Chodorow, Poland; and the Rashi Chapel in Worms, Germany). Great care was taken to ensure complete accuracy and authenticity, as can be judged from the colour photographs of the models in this volume, which are virtually indistinguishable from the original.

The ensuing chapters take the reader not only into the story of the design and architecture of the synagogue but also into the world it contained as the hub of the Jewish community around which revolved a beehive of activities. Here the Jew lived much of his life, dreamed his dreams, and communed with both God and his neighbour. In Hebrew it was called 'House of Prayer', 'House of Study' and 'House of Assembly' and it always sustained its threefold function. Within its friendly atmosphere, the Jew has always drawn sustenance and inspiration to face the often hostile world.

The author would like to thank Tamar Manor, who researched the illustrations; Uri Ram, the chief editor; David Cassuto, who gave invaluable advice on the Italian synagogues; and David Silber, Deputy Director of Beth Hatefutsoth, who conceived the project and was responsible for its execution.

- 1 -

tbe Beginnings

THE institution of the synagogue is unquestionably ancient, but just how ancient is a subject for speculation and scholarly dispute. It must have come into existence to answer a deeply-felt need, but nobody is sure of the circumstances which engendered its actual emergence. The most widespread and probable theory is that it was a product of the Babylonian exile. In the sixth century BC the Babylonians conquered the kingdom of Judah, destroyed the Temple built by Solomon in Jerusalem, and deported a large section of the population to Babylonia. Unlike their brothers, the Ten Tribes in the northern kingdom of Israel who had been deported 150 years earlier, the exiles of Judah did not assimilate into the surrounding population. On the contrary, they sat 'by the waters of Babylon and wept', bemoaning their lost homeland, their destroyed Temple and its elaborate ritual, the paramount expression of their faith.

The Jews found themselves in a religious vacuum which required a revolutionary re-ordering of their method of communion with God. The answer may have come spontaneously from the people; or it may have been inspired by the élite, perhaps even by the great exilic prophets, Ezekiel and the author of the second part of the Book of Isaiah. The exiles, it has been surmised, convened informally on the Sabbath and the holy festival days. These may have been the occasions on which they visited the prophets and other religious leaders, seeking consolation ('Comfort ye, comfort ye, my people') and encouragement in their hope for the return to Zion. It may have been here that their leaders expounded the scriptures, especially the Pentateuch, which had been accepted as holy. It may be that under these circumstances prayers were formulated – expressions of confession and repentance and petitions to God to restore the exiles to their homes and permit them to rebuild the Temple (envisioned in detail by Ezekiel). It has been suggested that Ezekiel's reference to 'a little sanctuary' (Ezekiel 11:16) refers to these incipient synagogues. In all events, the phrase became a common appellation for the synagogue in later Judaism.

Some scholars date the first synagogues to an earlier period, to the days of the First Temple. They claim that ancient rabbis, anxious to endow the institution with authority, ascribed its foundation to Moses. This view was popular in the first century AD when it was mentioned by both the historian Josephus and the New Testament ('For from early generations Moses has had in every city those who preach him, for he is read every Sabbath in the synagogues', Acts 15:21). One rabbinical

Masada, aerial view. On this rocky mountain in the Judean Desert near the Dead Sea, in the first century BC, Herod built a palace with a complex of other buildings, including a synagogue.
(Photo: Avraham Hai)

legend even relates that when Rebekah was pregnant with Esau and Jacob she noticed that whenever she passed a pagan temple Esau moved in her body, and whenever she passed a synagogue Jacob tried to break out of her womb.

Various passages of the Bible were interpreted as referring to the synagogue, but these references have been taken by scholars as indications of the existence of some form of prayer meeting held at the time of the First Temple particularly outside Jerusalem. The theory is that while pilgrims went to Jerusalem for the festivals many others remained behind and must have enjoyed some form of religious experience. Hence the Jews exiled to Babylon already took with them the rudimentary elements of synagogue practice. Those who hold this view maintain that when the exiles returned to Judah they kept up the tradition of the prayer meetings even though the Temple had been rebuilt. The Talmudic rabbis attributed the beginning of regular services to the men of the Great Assembly, the supreme religious institution of the post-exilic era, and it would seem likely that the activities of Ezra and Nehemiah and their successors, who were disseminating Torah, increased the need to establish special places throughout the land for prayer and Torah readings. Some scholars, however, arguing from different premises, including the fact that there is no mention of synagogues in any early source, claim that they came into being only at a later period.

The earliest reliable reference to a Jewish house of prayer comes from Egypt in the third century BC. It was natural that the Jews living in the Diaspora, for whom access to the Temple was difficult, felt the need for a place of assembly and worship. This evidence comes from an inscription found at Schedia, fifteen miles from Alexandria, commemorating the dedication of a Jewish place of prayer to the Egyptian ruler, Ptolemy III. From the same period there is another inscription indicating that a synagogue in lower Egypt had been given the right of asylum, a right granted to import-ant temples of other faiths. The synagogue must have appeared revolutionary – or at least eccentric – at a time when the pagan temples were conceived as the habitation of the deity, and when shrines were accessible only to the priestly caste and worship expressed through sacrifice.

Architecturally, the pagan houses of worship were not the chief influence on the early Diaspora synagogues. Indeed, a deliberate effort would probably have been made to avoid imitating the pagans. Their model was more likely community buildings of the Graeco-Roman world: large assembly halls with smaller halls for the conduct of legal business. The synagogue must have posed a challenge to its designers as it was the first religious centre catering to a congregation rather than to a priestly élite.

There is ample evidence that synagogues existed throughout the Diaspora by the first century AD. The greatest Jewish centre outside the Land of Israel was the metropolis of Alexandria, with its dozens of synagogues. Most famous was its Great Synagogue with seventy-one chairs of gold, for the elders of the community council, and its unusual seating arrangements: 'goldsmiths on their own, silversmiths on their own, blacksmiths on their own'. The basilica hall was so vast that the reader could not be heard at its extremities, and a special assistant waved a flag to indicate to the congregation when to respond 'Amen' to the blessings. 'He who has never seen the double stoa of the Great Synagogue in Alexandria has never seen the glory of Israel', ran the saying. Legend had it that it held twice the number of Jews who left Egypt in the Exodus. The synagogue was burned to the ground in the Jewish uprising against the Roman authorities in AD 115–17.

In the Roman Empire the Jews were not compelled to subscribe to the imperial religion but their exemption depended on their belonging to a community, of which the synagogue was the physical expression. The word 'synagogue' comes from the Greek for 'place of gathering' (which is also the meaning of the Hebrew term *Bet Knesset*), indicating that from the outset it was a multi-purpose institution, serving as a communal centre as well as a place of worship.

Wherever Jews lived in the later Second Temple period they founded their synagogues. This is shown most vividly in the New Testament account of the travels of Paul, who made a point of starting his visit to any city by going to the synagogue. There, as a guest, he would be invited to preach. He began preaching in the synagogue of Damascus and continued in Salamis in Cyprus, in Antioch of Pisidia, Iconium, Thessalonica, Berea, Corinth and Ephesus (in the Greece and Turkey of today). In most of these places his message was not favourably received, and his visits often ended in quarrels and even in violence. But the account demonstrates the role of the synagogue in the outlying communities of his day.

Thirteen synagogues are known to have existed in Rome, one of which was reputed to have had a Torah scroll brought from Jerusalem. The Emperor Augustus passed a law stipulating that theft from a synagogue was the equivalent of the theft of sacred objects. In gratitude for the Emperor's sympathetic attitude, some of the synagogues in Rome were named after him. There were, however, periods of tension and persecution as well, such as when the mad Emperor Caligula ordered his image to be placed in all houses of worship, including the synagogues.

The synagogue developed rapidly throughout the Diaspora and also in Palestine, where the Temple and synagogue existed side by side in harmony and with a clear division of function. The Jew went to the Temple to seek forgiveness for his sins; he went to the synagogue to offer his personal supplications and to listen to expositions of sacred literature. During this period the entire Jewish population was divided into groups of twenty-four, each group in attendance for a week in the Temple during the daily sacrifice. But as space was limited, in actuality only a token representa-

tion could participate. Those Israelites in each group who remained at home celebrated by attending special services in their towns and villages. These were held at the same time as the offering of the sacrifices in the Temple. Thus there must already have been daily morning and afternoon services, with extra ones on the Sabbath and festival days, to coincide with those in the Temple.

The New Testament provides further evidence of the central role of the synagogue in the provincial communities in Palestine since it was to the synagogues in Galilee that Jesus gravitated to address the assembled, especially on the Sabbath. It is recorded that the synagogue at Capernaum was built thanks to a sympathetic Roman centurion (Luke 7:5).

The synagogues were not confined to the provinces but flourished even in Jerusalem, in the shade of the Temple. (One Talmudic tradition reported 394 synagogues in Jerusalem prior to the destruction of the Temple but this is probably an exaggeration, even allowing for their usual small size.) There was a synagogue on the Temple Mount itself, linked to the Temple. The Mishna tells us that on the most solemn day in the Jewish calendar, the Day of Atonement, 'the synagogue official took the Torah scroll and handed it to the chief of the synagogue who handed it to the prefect, who in turn handed it to the High Priest, who received it and read from it, while standing'. It is related of one famous rabbi that he celebrated the Water Drawing ceremony on the Feast of Tabernacles 'between sacrifices in the Temple and prayers in the synagogue'. Moreover, every morning, after the completion of the sacrifices, the priests went to the Chamber of Hewn Stone (which was the seat of the Sanhedrin) for the recitation of the Ten Commandments, the *Shema* and additional benedictions – the original nucleus of the morning prayer.

Literary sources mention the fact that pilgrims to Jerusalem were often accommodated in the synagogues, and dramatic confirmation of the siting of an ancient synagogue there was given this century, with the discovery of the

'Theodotus inscription' in the City of David, dating from the first century AD. It notes that Theodotus built the synagogue for the reading of the Torah and for the teaching of the Commandments, as well as for a hospice. No remains of the synagogue itself were discovered (apart from some underground structures, possibly cisterns) and so for evidence of how synagogues looked in this period we have to go outside Jerusalem. Two exciting discoveries have been made in recent years in the excavated palaces of King Herod, one in Masada in the Judean Desert near the Dead Sea, the other at Herodion, near Bethlehem. Both sites were significantly occupied twice: once in the time of Herod in the first century BC, and for the second time a century later, when they were converted by Jewish Zealots into fortresses for the last desperate stand against the Roman armies. In both places archaeologists uncovered halls which they were able to identify as synagogues, of almost identical size (50 ft × about 40 ft). It was clear that the Zealots, who were deeply nationalistic and religious, had used these halls as synagogues, but since in Masada there was evidence of an earlier building on the same site, it seems probable that there had been a synagogue there in the time of Herod as well. If so, this would be the earliest synagogue building ever uncovered. Between the two periods the Masada site was occupied by the Romans, and from the remains of dung the excavators surmised that they used it as a stable.

Below: Greek inscription from a Jerusalem synagogue prior to the destruction of the Second Temple: 'Theodotos son of Vettenos, priest and leader of the synagogue [*archisynagogos*], son and grandson of a synagogue leader, built the synagogue for reciting the law and studying the commandments; and the hospice, the rooms and the water installations to house travellers from abroad. The synagogue was founded by his father with the elders and Simonidus.'
(*Israel Department of Antiquities, Jerusalem*)

Opposite: Synagogue at Masada, built into the casemate wall of the fortress, constructed by the Zealots and besieged by the Romans, *c.*AD 70. It was built partly from remnants of Herod's palace and is located over the earlier synagogue built by Herod. The rows of benches around the walls are clearly visible, as are the bases of the columns. The secondary room on the left may have been used for storing ritual objects, including Torah scrolls.
(*Photo: Avraham Hai*)

In Herod's time the hall at Masada had been divided in two, comprising an entrance hall and a sanctuary. The Zealots removed the partition between the two rooms to enlarge the sanctuary but they also added another small room. The main hall in the Zealot synagogue had two rows of columns and three rows of benches along the walls. The benches were made from stones taken from Herod's palaces and plastered with clay. The identification of the hall as a synagogue was strengthened by the discovery of two pits containing fragments of biblical scrolls. Already in those days, damaged or worn out scriptures were not destroyed but stored in a depository (*geniza* in Hebrew) often located in the synagogue. Portions of the Bible scrolls were discovered under the Masada synagogue, one of which was particularly significant. It was Ezekiel's Vision of the Dry Bones, which prophesied the revival of the exiled Jewish people and their return to Zion.

The Zealots in Herodion had similarly adapted the ancient hall, adding columns and three rows of benches along the walls, also constructed from the remains of Herod's palaces. In both places the halls were simple and without ornamentation. The Zealots were an austere group and since their primary objective was to fortify themselves against the Romans, the artistic decoration of their beloved

synagogue was probably of little import to them. Their military preoccupations notwithstanding, they strictly observed the obligations of ritual purity and constructed in both places a ritual bath close to the synagogue.

The orientation of these synagogues is not clear. Some believe they faced Jerusalem but another suggestion is that in Second Temple Times they faced east, in accordance with an early rabbinical ordinance that synagogues should have their entrances (and presumably also their orientation) to the east because that was where the entrance was in the Temple. This latter theory holds that the orientation towards Jerusalem was introduced only after the destruction of the Temple. However, this

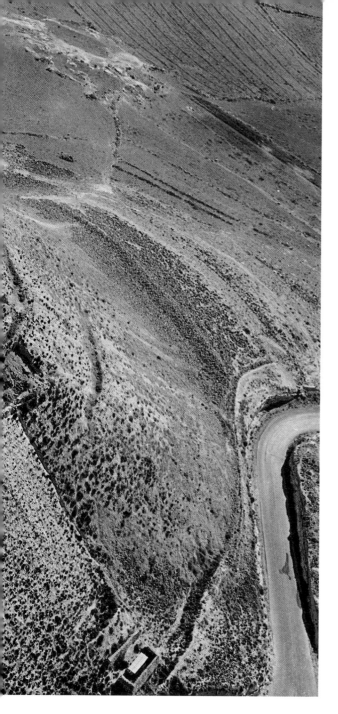

seems to be refuted by a recent discovery at Gamla on the Golan Heights, near the Syrian border. The large, elongated hall with its rows of benches along the wall and nearby ritual bath was most probably a synagogue dating from the time of the Second Temple (it was destroyed in AD 66–7 during the Roman War). But here the entrance is to the west and the orientation is towards Jerusalem. So the determination of systematic regulations on the positioning of these early synagogues remains controversial.

The building at Gamla seems to be the only one from this period found so far which was constructed specifically as a synagogue. Moreover, unlike the remote fortresses of Masada and Herodion, it was built inside a town, for a community. The main sanctuary has four rows of columns, one along each side, so that the central nave is surrounded by four

Above: Herodion, aerial view. On this rocky ground near Bethlehem in the Judean Desert, Herod constructed a palace and fortress similar to that of Masada, but on a smaller scale.
(*Photo: Avraham Hai*)

Right: Synagogue (*left*) at Herodion, built by the Zealots who defended the mountain against the Romans in AD 70. To the right is the entrance to the ritual bath.
(*Courtesy of Gideon Foerster, Jerusalem*)

aisles. The Torah scroll was kept in a recess in the wall and was brought into the prayer area during services. Here, and in the other synagogues mentioned, there is no evidence that men and women were separated. The building was erected, not put up under pressure, and the opportunity was taken to adorn it. Among the motifs are petalled rosettes and date palms, common features of early Jewish art.

From the literary and archaeological evidence it is clear that wherever Jews lived at the end of the Second Temple period, they had their synagogues. This was to prove crucial for them, both in surviving the destruction of the Temple and in reconstructing Jewish worship after this traumatic event.

Synagogue at Gamla on the Golan Heights, probably erected in the late first century BC – early first century AD. This is the only known urban synagogue dating from the era of the Second Temple. Stone benches line its four walls. It was presumably destroyed during or after the Roman siege of AD 67.
(*Photo: Danny Friedman*)

the classical period

THE Temple, the focus of Jewish ritual for a thousand years, was destroyed, for the second time, by the Romans in AD 70. As in the period after its destruction by the Babylonians, the Jews dreamt of its restoration and their prayers were filled with such hopes. But realistically they had to adapt to a completely new set of circumstances, and the rabbinical authorities, from their new seat in Yavneh, redesigned the nature of Jewish worship, centring it on the synagogue. They institutionalized the correspondence of the times of prayers with the former sacrifices; they transferred the priestly blessing and the Levitical psalm of the day to the liturgy; they brought many Temple rituals into the synagogue – such as the sounding of the *shofar* and the Tabernacles procession of the four species; and they incorporated recollections and descriptions of the sacrificial system into the prayers. Indeed, prayer was defined as a substitute for sacrifice and was called 'the sacrifice of the heart'. The rabbis formulated clear guidelines for three daily prayers with extra services on the Sabbath and festivals. The synagogue patterns, prayer forms and liturgies laid down at that time have remained constant to this day. A Jew of the first century would find himself at home in a synagogue of the twentieth century. Moreover, the synagogue was suited to the enforced exile and wanderings of the Jewish people. Unlike the Temple it was not anchored in a specific place and could accompany the Jews wherever they made their homes. By the first century the basic functions of the synagogue had been crystallized: it was primarily a house of prayer.

But just as Jewishness also has ethnic and cultural implications, so the synagogue assumed more extensive roles than those relating to worship.

The synagogue building was now the main communal assembly hall as well as the classroom, both for children and for adults who gathered to listen to expositions of Scriptures and rabbinical literature. It also served as the temporary depository for funds gathered from the community for a variety of purposes. Rich coin finds have been made under the ruins of synagogues in Caesarea, and in Merot in eastern Galilee. In Merot the treasure was found in a collection box carved in the floor of a storeroom attached to the synagogue. The hole in the floor was stopped by a stone plug, which fitted so tightly that it escaped notice after the building was abandoned. Five hundred coins were found there, half of them gold.

For over a century after the Jewish revolt of AD 66–70, and especially after the second revolt against the Romans in 132–5, the Jews in Palestine were severely oppressed and the building of synagogues was impossible. But towards the end of the second century the Roman attitude relaxed, relations with the Jewish community became more peaceful, the economic situation improved, and the next century saw a spate of building. The Jews at this time could build monumental houses of worship and many of them, especially those in Galilee, have now been excavated. The earliest discoveries were made in the mid-nineteenth century by non-Jews, one of whom was

Herbert Kitchener (better known for his military exploits as 'Kitchener of Khartoum' and as Britain's Secretary of State for War in the First World War). He came across eleven synagogues in Galilee and suggested that the Roman emperors must have inspired and assisted in their construction contributing Roman labour. 'The Jews themselves', he wrote in 1878, 'having taken to commercial pursuits were unable to perform work of this sort and by using Roman workmen obtained much finer results than we are led to think they themselves would have been capable of'. A century of intensive research has, however, pointed to very different conclusions.

More than one hundred synagogues have been discovered in Israel so far, dating from between the third and eighth centuries AD. They are situated in all parts of the country, reflecting the widespread extent of Jewish settlement. The earliest major body of synagogues was scattered throughout Galilee, which was the main centre of Jewish habitation after the destruction of the Temple. They have much in common architecturally and artistically, and a general line of development can be discerned although scholars are disputing the theories of classification.

Rabbinical precept taught that a synagogue should be built on the highest point in the area or near a body of water. The Galilean synagogues often command breathtaking views and their great height sometimes required the construction of a platform or steps for access. There are synagogues near large bodies of water (such as the one at Capernaum on the shores of the Sea of Galilee) and near brooks or springs, the proximity of water being particularly useful for purification rituals.

Many of the earlier synagogues are of distinguished appearance and consist basically of a main prayer hall and a courtyard. They were constructed when the Romans ruled the country, and the halls were inspired by the Roman basilica. Two rows of columns divided the hall into a broad central nave with two narrow aisles (in some a third row of columns, built

Façade of the synagogue at Baram in Galilee (third century AD), with its three entrances and the lower part of the second storey.
(*Government Press Office, Tel Aviv*)

crossways, provided a third aisle). The façade was elaborate and characterized by three entrances: a large door in the centre opened into the nave with the two smaller doors on either side leading into the aisles. A large window often surmounted the central entrance. The most impressive façade still preserved is from the synagogue at Baram near the Lebanese frontier. Built of basalt masonry, it rises to a height of twenty feet and contains the three

period (fourth to sixth centuries), the more logical step was taken of making the entrance in the northern wall so that upon entering the worshipper would immediately be facing south, towards Jerusalem, and latecomers would enter at the back of the congregation.

The ground plans varied according to circumstances. The first consideration was topographical, and some of the variations for which scholars sought ideological or religious explanations were simply due to the lie of the land. Financial resources were another determining factor and short-cuts would inevitably have been taken when money grew scarce. The architects were subject to outside influence and had presumably studied under non-Jewish masters, perhaps in Syrian schools of architecture (or they themselves may have been non-Jews). And so we find echoes of Graeco-Roman architecture in the earlier buildings with their columns; of the art forms prevalent in Syria; and of Christian art and architecture of the time in the Byzantine period. Nevertheless, some of the synagogues discovered (such as those at Eshtemoa and Susiya in Judea) fit into no known category, while the special requirements of Jewish worship also evoked original solutions affecting the design of the buildings. Moreover, the workmen, the masons and the stonecutters, many of whom are known to have been Jews, were given considerable leeway and used their initiative to introduce local elements and customs.

The early synagogues in Galilee had imposing exteriors, built with large, hewn stones sometimes ten feet long, but their interiors were unpretentious, designed in such a way that the worshipper could concentrate on his devotions without distraction. The only rich ornamentation was a frieze running round the gallery. The basic pattern was geometric but plant, animal and even human forms were introduced into these reliefs and into the exterior designs (although later, under the iconoclastic interpretation of the second Commandment, the human likenesses were obliterated).

doors, a portico with four columns before the main entrance, and is the only surviving synagogue where a second storey is still visible.

The first Galilean synagogues faced south, towards Jerusalem. As the entrance was also on the south side, the worshipper had to turn 180 degrees after entering the sanctuary in order to face the direction of prayer. This must have proved a distraction for those already at prayer and at a later stage, in the Byzantine

Top: Partially reconstructed remains of the white limestone synagogue at Capernaum (about third or fourth century AD). Benches line two walls on the left. (*Photo: Avraham Hai*)

Above: Carved stone frieze from the synagogue at Capernaum. The six-pointed star (*left*) had no special Jewish significance at that time. (*Government Press Office, Tel Aviv*)

Detail of decoration outside the synagogue at Capernaum depicting the Ark of the Covenant on a wagon. (*Government Press Office, Tel Aviv*)

The most strikingly preserved and subsequently restored of the ancient synagogues is at Capernaum (Kfar Nahum). This is not the one mentioned in the New Testament as the place where Jesus preached but a later one, possibly built on the same site. Scholars are divided as to its exact date: some say it was constructed in the second or third century, others in the fourth or fifth. Set in an area where all building was in the local black basalt, its bright white limestone, brought from quite some distance, must have provided a dazzling contrast to the surroundings. Its richly-decorated two-storey façade faced Jerusalem and its interior was a classical basilica with three colonnaded porticoes. Around its walls were two rows of benches which may have been reserved for the more distinguished members of the congregation, the others sitting on mats on the floor. At one corner of the hall is an annexe, presumably used for storing Torah scrolls and possibly as a hostel.

The Christian Byzantines, who ruled the Eastern Roman Empire including Palestine from the fourth century, introduced harsh anti-Jewish laws, with a ban on building new synagogues. Even when the laws were relaxed and new ones could be constructed, the Jews deemed it expedient to avoid external ostentation. The exteriors became much simpler and the hewn stone gave way to a plastered, undressed stone. Artistic compensation was obtained by more elaborate interiors. Most strikingly, the former simple flagstones of the floor gave way to colourful 'wall-to-wall' mosaics, emulating the contemporary Byzantine churches. Apart from geometric designs, the mosaics that have been discovered portray three main groups of subjects: conventional Jewish symbols (the candelabrum, the ram's horn, the four species used on the Feast of Tabernacles and the Torah shrine); the signs of the zodiac and even themes inspired by Greek mythology (in a floor found at Gaza, King David is portrayed as Orpheus playing the lyre); and scenes from the Bible, often conveying the hope for redemption, such as

Noah's ark, the sacrifice of Isaac, or Daniel in the lion's den. The mosaic at Nirim in southern Israel is devoted to a wide range of animals. No restrictions were observed concerning the depiction of human figures and apparently no qualms were felt in treading on biblical imagery, which even included the representation of the hand of God reaching down from the heavens. A rabbinical source specifically permitted figures and likenesses in the floor, as long as the worshipper did not prostrate himself on them. Sometimes inscriptions in Hebrew, Aramaic or Greek were incorporated, containing the names of the artist or donor. Striking mosaics have been discovered in various parts of the country, from Beth Alfa in the north to Nirim in the south.

Mosaic from the synagogue at Bet Alfa, Jezreel Valley (sixth century AD). In the centre, the wheel of the zodiac with Helios. In the foreground, the sacrifice of Isaac. On the left, Abraham's two attendants; the ram entangled in the bush; Abraham offering up Isaac. Above, the hand of God reaches down from heaven.
(*Photo: Avraham Hai*)

Right: Drawing of the mosaic floor of the synagogue at Maon near Nirim in southern Israel (sixth century). At the top, a *menora* (candelabrum) with citrons, a ram's horn, palm branches and two lions. Below, medallions with a variety of animals. The Aramaic inscription above the mosaic honours three individual donors. (*From 'Bulletin of the Louis M.Rabinowitz Fund', No. 3, Jerusalem, December 1960*)

Opposite: Mosaic floor of the synagogue at Hammath-Tiberias (third to fourth century AD), broken by a wall added later. In the centre, the wheel of the zodiac with the Greek sun-god, Helios; above, the ark of the Torah; below, two lions flank Greek inscriptions honouring the builders (*Photo: Avraham Hai*)

Below: Detail of the synagogue mosaic at Gaza (reconstructed) portraying King David as Orpheus, playing his lyre, dressed as a Byzantine emperor (early sixth century AD). (*Music and Ethnography Museum, Haifa*)

One of the questions debated by scholars is whether, in the early synagogues, women were separated from men for prayer. The so-called 'Women's Court' in the Temple was attended by men as well, and there is no clear statement in early rabbinical literature enjoining the segregation of women. Some of the synagogues, such as those at Capernaum and Baram, had a gallery which it was assumed was for women, but this surmise has been questioned. In synagogues lacking a gallery no special provision was made for women, and many scholars believe that the separation of women was a comparatively late development.

One of the chief keys to understanding the chronological development of the synagogue buildings throughout this period is the provision made for the Torah scroll. At first none was made: the scroll or scrolls were kept in a portable chest in an adjoining room and brought in for services. (It has been suggested that the central of the three doors in the façade may have been reserved for bringing in the Torah scrolls.) The next stage was the construction of a niche in the hall in front of the main entrance in which the scroll was placed during prayers. It was appropriately decorated, as a rule, although it is not clear whether the scroll was left permanently inside the synagogue or brought in only when appropriate. In the course of time (between the fourth and eighth centuries) the wall facing Jerusalem was developed into an apse, usually in the shape of a semicircle. Here the Torah scroll found a permanent home, probably behind a curtain or screen (sometimes made of marble), to be taken out and placed in its shrine during the service. The apse was raised and access was up a few steps (similar platforms could be found in church apses at that time.)

Synagogues have been discovered throughout the entire area of ancient Palestine, including Transjordan. Since 1967 intensive work has been carried out in excavating remains of synagogues in the Golan Heights. A homogeneous type has been identified, with certain resemblances to the Galilean synagogues, but with unique architectural and artistic features. These are partly due to the extreme hardness of the local basalt which necessitated special techniques. The synagogues date from the fifth or sixth century, and provide evidence of a dense Jewish habitation of the region. The similarities with those in Palestine seem to stem from a common source of influence, probably in southern Syria. They all had monumental façades with a single ornamental entrance. Variety was to be found in the decorative schemes, perhaps because of a stronger oriental influence, the style of low relief (necessitated by the nature of the stone), and the subject-matter which concentrated on fauna while eschewing mythology.

During this entire period, up to the sixth century, the Jewish Diaspora was expanding in every direction. Jews reached Spain in the west,

Mosaic floor from the synagogue of the Byzantine period at En-Gedi, on the Dead Sea, depicting peacocks eating grapes, the words 'Peace for Israel' and several inscriptions. One of these invokes a curse on anyone 'who causes dissension between one man and another, who slanders his fellow-Jews to the Gentiles, who steals the property of his fellows, or reveals the town's secrets to Gentiles.'
(*Government Press Office, Tel Aviv*)

Detail of the Bet Alfa mosaic panel, located in front of the Torah shrine; it contains a representation of the ark, with a gabled roof, seen through an open curtain. The ark is flanked on either side by a seven-branched candelabrum traditional religious objects – *shofars*, *lulav*, *ethrog* and an incense shovel.
(*Photo: Avraham Hai*)

Above: A stone from the village of En Samsam in the Golan Heights which seems to have originated in the synagogue at En Neshut, where it formed the base of the Torah shrine.
(*Courtesy of Zvi Maoz, Katzrin*)

Below: Remains of the Golan's best-preserved synagogue, at Katzrin (*c.* fifth century AD). It was partially destroyed in the seventh century; in the thirteenth century one section was turned into a mosque.
(*Government Press Office, Tel Aviv*)

Persia and beyond in the east, the Rhineland in the north and Arabia and Yemen in the south. Wherever Jews lived they built their synagogues, deeply and unavoidably influenced by the art and architecture of their surroundings. There must have been many such buildings but so far the number of those discovered is much fewer than in Palestine. It was not to be expected that they would resemble each other nor show obvious similarites to the synagogues in Palestine. But what they do have in common is their orientation towards Jerusalem and the same Jewish symbols in their decorations. Apart from the archaeological evidence, there is information on synagogues in literary sources. The Babylonian Talmud, for example, contains extensive information on the synagogues in Babylonia, of which no material remains have been discovered. A synagogue as far away as Orléans in France was destroyed in the sixth century. And there is the impassioned call of the anti-Jewish Church Father, John Chrysostom, in 386, condemning Christians (especially women) in Antioch, for choosing to attend synagogues on Jewish festivals.

Some of the earliest synagogues discovered are in Greece and Asia Minor. Controversy has raged over the identification of a building in Delos, but if it is indeed a synagogue, it is the earliest one known in the Diaspora, dating from the period before the destruction of the Temple. Another early synagogue may have been located at Corinth where an inscription was found, probably from the lintel, saying 'Synagogue of the Hebrews', together with the upper part of a column – a capital – adorned with three seven-branched candelabra and the four species. Synagogues in Asia Minor were found in Miletus (a three-colonnaded basilica dating from the third or fourth century), and Priene (converted from a private dwelling in the fourth or fifth century). The synagogue in Aegina in the Gulf of Piraeus, dating from the fifth or sixth century, does bear some resemblance to the Palestinian synagogues of its time – such as its apse and its mosaic floor.

Early synagogues have also been found in Syria, Yugoslavia, the Crimea, and apparently also in Spain. Those in Rome are known from literary sources when they became the target of vicious attacks. After the Christianization of the Empire they were looted, burned, or turned into churches. When the Emperor complained, the famous bishop of Milan, St Ambrose,

Capital with three candelabra from the synagogue at
Corinth (fourth to sixth century AD).
(*Courtesy of Gideon Foerster, Jerusalem*)

Plaque from the Priene synagogue with candelabra and
other Jewish symbols. The curling lines under the
candelabrum branches may have represented furled
Torah scrolls.
(*From T. Wieg and M. Schrader, 'Priene, Ergebnisse der
Ausgrabungen', Berlin 1904*)

expressed the regret that he had not himself
had the opportunity of setting fire to a
synagogue.

Some of these buildings call for particular
consideration. The most majestic was discovered at Sardis in western Turkey, the capital
of ancient Lydia, and was excavated in the
1960s. Sardis had an estimated population of
100,000 in Roman times. The first-century
historian, Josephus, made a reference to its
Jewish community and its 'place of assembly',
guaranteed 'according to their ancestral laws'.
The building was erected in the first century,
but not initially for Jewish purposes. It formed
part of a complex in the centre of the city which
included the baths and a gymnasium, and
adjoined a row of shops (many of them run by
Jews) along the city's main street. The basilica,
which is almost four hundred feet long and
which was initially used for some civic purpose, was given to the Jewish community to be
used as a house of prayer and assembly, and for
this purpose it was remodelled to some extent.
Its final form seems to date from the fourth
century, but it is not clear when it first became a
synagogue. It consisted of two main sections.
The forecourt, probably used as an assembly
hall, had a huge marble laver, probably for the

ritual washing of hands. Three doors led from
it into the enormous hall of the synagogue
which had accommodation for over a thousand
worshippers. At the eastern end was an apse,
probably part of the original building, with
bench seating for seventy (presumably the
elders of the community). The Torah scrolls
were not kept in the apse but seemed to have
been stored on the opposite side, between two
of the doors leading from the forecourt. Facing
the apse was a huge marble table, with legs
shaped like eagles, probably used for readings,
flanked on either side by the statue of a lion.
There are indications that the reader's platform might have stood in the middle of the hall.
The floors were mosaics of geometric patterns,
while the walls either had marble decorations
or were painted. The building contains a dozen
depictions of candelabra as well as the remains
of a marble candelabrum, which must have
been four feet wide. It contained an inscription
bearing the name 'Socrates'. Eighty inscriptions in the floor, mostly in Greek, give information on other members of the congregation
and on donors, including a number of women.
(There is no sign in the building of separate
accommodation for women.)

While Sardis is the most impressive ancient

synagogue, architecturally speaking, Dura-Europos (Dura was the original Assyrian name, Europos, the later Seleucid name), on the Euphrates in Syria, is the most remarkable from an artistic point of view. The remains of this remote frontier town were discovered by chance in 1920 when British soldiers, digging a trench, came across evidence of the Roman occupation. The synagogue had been saved by sheer luck. In the year 256, expecting an attack by the Persians, the Romans had built a massive ramp to reinforce the defences of the town. As the synagogue backed on to the street adjoining the city wall, it was surrounded and protected by the ramp: not only was the building saved but its paintings were wonderfully preserved for almost seventeen centuries. The excavation revealed that two synagogues had existed on the site. They were modest mud-brick buildings, situated in a residential district with access through a forecourt. The first may have been erected in the late second century but the second synagogue was definitely completed in AD 244 (as evidenced by an inscription), and so was in use for only a dozen years before it was incorporated into the ramp. There was seating accommodation for about 120, with no special provision for women. The surprise of this discovery was the richness and nature of the decorations: all four walls were painted in tempera with depictions of incidents from the Bible, while the tiles on the ceiling between the beams were painted with geometric designs. All the walls were divided into five levels but the top section, which had protruded above the ramp, was destroyed. The lowest level consists largely of animal and human forms, while the other three contain scenes from the Bible, fifty-eight episodes in all. Human figures are freely displayed; even the eastern wall, which the congregation faced, shows the Pharaoh's daughter bathing nude in the Nile. As in Beth Alfa, the anthropomorphic hand of God reaches down from the heavens in several of the scenes. The Torah shrine is embedded in a conch above which are shown the sacrifice of Isaac and typical Jewish symbols including,

Outer courtyard (*atrium*) of the synagogue at Sardis with the large marble laver.
(*Beth Hatefutsoth Archive, Tel Aviv*)

Above: Forecourt of the synagogue at Sardis looking towards the entrance to the prayer hall. This forecourt may have been used for community assemblies. The marble laver in the centre was originally a fountain.
(*Beth Hatefutsoth model/Photo: Michael Horton*)

Opposite, above: The synagogue at Sardis, 60 miles from the west coast of Turkey, discovered in 1962. It was originally built in the first century AD as a Roman basilica. In the foreground is the apse with three rows of benches for the elders of the community. Beyond that is a marble table, probably used for Torah readings. Towards the back of the hall are the bases of four pillars which may have supported the reader's desk. At the far end are three entrances with shrines between them which may have been used for storing the Torah scrolls. The building was destroyed when the city fell to the Persians in AD 616.
(*Beth Hatefutsoth model/Photo: Michael Horton*)

Right: Synagogue at Dura-Europos in Syria, on the banks of the Euphrates. The synagogue, excavated in 1928–32, was completed in AD 244–5. Its most remarkable features are the paintings of biblical scenes and other illustrations along all four walls. The ceiling was constructed of elaborately painted tiles. Benches for seating were along the bottom of all the walls. The original is preserved in the Damascus Museum. (*Beth Hatefutsoth model/Photo: Michael Horton*)

apparently, an imaginary representation of the Temple. Various ingenious theories have been proposed to explain the selection and arrangement of the subjects: one insists that they are of Messianic significance; another claims a mystical motivation; and a third that the three panels represent respectively historical, liturgical and moral themes. What is certain is that it has thrown new light on the attitude of the ancient Jews to art. Moreover, this chance find would seem to imply that this was not an exceptional case but must have been one of many.

The first synagogue found in Italy was discovered in 1961 at Ostia, the ancient port of Rome. Part of the building was constructed in the first century but its final form dates from the fourth. It is a basilica-type structure with three entrance doors (as in Galilee), an apse, and a mosaic floor. One unique aspect is an inner gateway, composed of four columns, leading to the shrine. An inscription, in Latin and Hebrew, records that 'For the Emperor's health, Mindis Faustos constructed the Ark of the Sacred Law at his own expense'. Jewish symbols are carved around the Tabernacle of the Ark. An original discovery for this era is the oven for baking *matzoth* (unleavened bread) in one of the adjoining rooms. Recently another synagogue has been discovered at Reggio di Calabria in the extreme south of Italy. It has been dated to the fourth century and was built

Left: Columns and lintel of the synagogue at Ostia, with Jewish symbols (candelabrum, ram's horn and the four species).
(*Beth Hatefutsoth Archive, Tel Aviv/Photo: Eddy Levy*)

Opposite: Palm tree from an idyllic scene (possibly of Paradise) in the Hammam-Lif Synagogue (fourth century).
(*Brooklyn Museum, New York*)

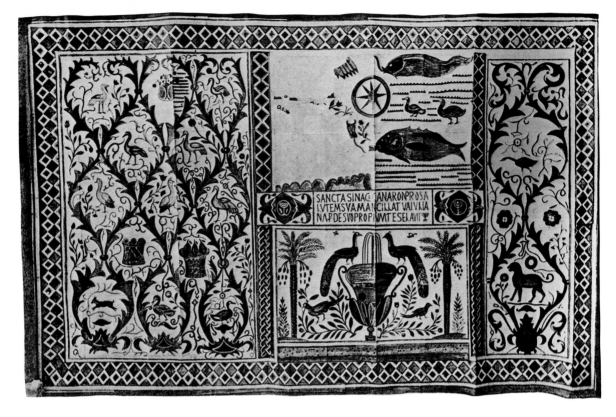

Drawing of the mosaic floor of the fourth-century synagogue at Hammam-Lif (Naro) in Tunisia. The rich variety of animals and plants includes two peacocks drinking from a fountain flanked by palm trees. Next to the Latin inscription are candelabra and other Jewish symbols.
(*Revue des études juives, XIII, 1886*)

over a second-century structure, probably also a synagogue. Its mosaic floor contained Jewish decorative motifs while a niche was designed to point towards Jerusalem.

Finally, mention should be made of the fourth-century synagogue discovered on the beach of Hammam-Lif at Naro in Tunisia, near ancient Carthage. Although hidden among private houses to lower its profile, it was a fifteen-room complex including a main prayer hall and a pillared courtyard (which may have served as an outdoor synagogue during the summer months). The inscriptions mention someone called Julia, who was one of the building's main benefactors and had the rich mosaic floor built 'at her own expense'. The focal point of the mosaic is two peacocks drinking at a fountain. They are flanked by palm trees, and a variety of animals amid floral decoration covers the rest of the mosaic. Since its discovery in 1884 fragments have been lost, but much of the mosaic is now in the Brooklyn Museum in New York.

The rich record of synagogues built both in the land of Israel and in the lands of the Diaspora comes to an end as we enter the 'Dark Ages', with the belligerent spread of Islam, on the one hand, and the aggressive anti-Jewish policies of the Church on the other. Jews living in either the Moslem or Christian orbit found themselves hard put to devote themselves to artistic creation, or to originality in the construction of houses of worship. It is only when we emerge from the tunnel of the Dark Ages that we find ourselves in a very different world.

3

MEDIEVAL EUROPE

IN the Middle Ages the Talmudic injunctions regarding synagogues came up against harsh reality: severe restrictions on Jews were imposed by their Christian and Moslem rulers. What had been eminently reasonable in the comparatively liberal circumstances prevailing in Palestine and Babylonia at the time when the two Talmuds were written was no longer so. Adjustments were necessary. For example, there was the injunction to build the synagogue on the highest spot in the area. (One Talmudic sage stated that 'any town where the house roofs are higher than the synagogue is doomed to destruction'.) This certainly could not be applied when the non-Jewish authorities insisted that synagogues be inconspicuous and under no circumstances higher than the church or the minaret. The Jews had no choice but to acquiesce. Nonetheless, they sought forms of compensation, even only symbolic, such as putting a pole or a rod on the roof of the synagogue to give it greater height.

In Babylonia it was the custom for synagogues to be built outside the city, since according to the rabbis cities were considered to be 'filled with unclean things'. Even in Babylonia this posed problems of safety. Consequently evening services were usually not held on weekdays, and on Friday evenings special prayers were added for the congregation so that latecomers could catch up in the recitation of the statutory service. In this way they were able to return to the city with the others and not make the potentially dangerous journey back on their own. In medieval Europe synagogues were always built inside the walls,

for Jews would have made too tempting a target walking alone outside the walls. The obvious location was within the Jewish quarter, despite the cramped conditions. There it was not only convenient but could be designed as the most impressive edifice in the neighbourhood without posing a challenge to other public buildings or churches. Problems did arise, however, if it was too close to the Christian quarter: some synagogues were ordered to be destroyed because the sound of the service reached a nearby church or chapel and disturbed the Christians in their worship.

The rabbis specified that ten Jews living in one place constituted a community and had to have a synagogue, but they did not regulate its external appearance and therefore Jews had no problem in adapting their places of worship to the surrounding architecture. In the words of one rabbi 'We have no prescribed form whatsoever for the shape of synagogues', although medieval sages issued warnings against innovations which merely imitated current fashions.

Stipulations were made concerning particular aspects. One was the obligation to incorporate windows, derived from the verse in the Book of Daniel (6:11): 'Daniel went into his house; now his windows were open in his upper chamber toward Jerusalem, and he kneeled three times a day and prayed.' Ideally, the rabbis said, there should be twelve windows, corresponding to the twelve tribes, but this could seldom be executed. At least one window, however, had to face Jerusalem. The entrance was not to be on the same side as the ark and, where possible, the worshipper had first to pass through a vestibule so as not to enter directly from the street. The congregation had to face in the direction of Jerusalem. Biblical sanction for this was found both in the quotation from Daniel and in Solomon's prayer at the dedication of the Temple (1 Kings 8:30): 'Hearken Thou to the supplication of Thy servant and of Thy people Israel when they pray toward this place'. The real reason for the Jerusalem orientation, however, was not Biblical injunction but rather the Zion-centredness of Judaism. All prayer services incorporated petitions for the end of the exile and the return of the Jewish people to their land. The early rabbis formulated the law: 'In the Diaspora, face the Land of Israel; in the Land of Israel, face Jerusalem; in Jerusalem face the Temple Mount.'

The ark was to be placed along the wall facing Jerusalem and the reader's platform (the *bima*) was to be in the centre of the hall so that the reader and preacher could be best heard by the entire congregation. This, however, was not obligatory and the planners could use their own discretion to place the platform at the end of the hall if they had good reason, especially if the synagogue was small and acoustics not problematic.

Even in ancient times the place of honour was along the wall where the ark was situated. The elders of the community sat here, facing the congregation but with their backs to Jerusalem, except during standing prayers when they turned in the same direction as the other congregants. It was an early tradition for worshippers to have fixed places, and by the Middle Ages the right to such a place was

German Jews at prayer, from a *siddur* (prayer-book) of Ashkenazi rite, 1471.
(*Bodleian Library, Oxford*)

regarded as part of the owner's assets. It could be sold and claimed by creditors in payment of debts; sometimes it was even sequestered by non-Jewish creditors who would then sell it by auction.

The rabbinical sources are permissive on the subject of synagogue art, although restrictions were imposed on representational art which might interfere with the concentration of the worshipper, who was enjoined to be totally oblivious of his surroundings while at prayer. Wall paintings were allowed. The Talmud even records the fact that there were outstanding rabbis in Nehardea in Babylonia who prayed in a synagogue which contained a human statue because, they said, the prayer was public and it was obvious that there could be no suspicion of idolatry. Differences of opinion, however, were recorded. Some rabbis allowed murals and mosaics; others felt that the money would be better spent on promoting scholarship. Under the impact of Islam in the Moslem lands and asceticism in Europe, the latter view prevailed and by the Middle Ages representational art was virtually absent from the synagogue.

In the early Middle Ages the main centre of Jewish habitation under Christian rule was the area known as Ashkenaz, mainly northern France and western Germany but extending, in fact, from England to Bohemia. The most important communities were in the Rhineland (especially Speyer, Worms, and Mainz) and it is there that we pick up the story of the synagogue. Centuries of persecution and expulsion, coupled with rigid religious attitudes and the prevailing poverty, precluded lavish building or decoration. (The government would sometimes punish a community by locking its synagogue or, if the Jews were being expelled, by turning it into a church.) Jews had no opportunity to develop original architecture and as they were excluded from the craft guilds, the actual architects were non-Jews who drew upon the existing styles, such as the Romanesque and Gothic which were prevalent in Europe at the time. In many places Jews were not allowed to own land, and therefore synagogues were held either on a short-term lease or by Christian trustees. The synagogues were unobtrusive in their exteriors and modest in their interiors in the hope that their anonymity would afford them some measure of safety against attack. In small communities the synagogue was nothing more than a small room set aside for prayer and suited to the needs of tradition. Few examples of interior decorations have survived. Medieval rabbis differed in their views of what subjects were suitable for artistic adornment. One authority ruled that the depiction of birds and horses was permitted and in the early synagogue of Regensburg, among others, the walls were covered with paintings of animals and plants. Yet the stained glass windows in the Cologne Synagogue were condemned by the rabbis for portraying snakes and lions, and objections were raised even to simple floral motifs. The school of German pietists known as the 'Hasidei Ashkenaz' frowned on artistic representation altogether. Moreover, the communities feared that embellishments would lead to accusations of extravagance by the authorities. Only in the late seventeenth century did the art of decoration flourish in German synagogues but this was after Jewish craftsmen fled the great massacres of 1648–9 in Poland, and then only in the small towns and villages in which they settled. Of the artistically crafted ritual objects, known from written sources to have been common, almost nothing has survived. This can be ascribed to the pillaging of synagogues, the expulsions of communities, and the need to raise funds for ransom or other purposes (not to mention the natural process of wear and tear).

Many synagogues in Europe were built below street level and the worshipper had to descend steps in order to enter. Homiletically, this was explained by Psalms 130:1: 'Out of the depths have I called to thee, O Lord' but it was more probably introduced for purely architectural considerations. As the height of the roof was limited by law, greater internal height was

achieved by sinking the floor.

Emphasis on the reader's platform as the focal point was a further architectural feature during this period. Artistic tension had always existed between the ark and the platform as the centre of interest and a balance between the two had to be maintained. Now, although the ark regained its holy and symbolic significance and had its fixed place, it was seen primarily as a place for storing the scrolls and indicating the direction of Jerusalem (by virtue of its position along the revered eastern wall). It was not, however, seen as an element affecting the design. The platform became the centre of attention, where things were happening, and as the hall, was used for non-religious functions, including being used as a place of assembly, it was the site of the platform which determined the design.

Another medieval development was the definite separation of the women's section from the prayer hall. In many cases it was an addition, not incorporated in the original

structure. The isolation of the women now became inflexibly enforced. Sometimes they were placed in a gallery (curtained out of view), and sometimes in an annexe to the main hall. The aperture was often so narrow that not only could they not see or be seen but they could not even hear the service. To help them follow, the women sometimes had their own prayer-leader (also a woman) who conducted the prayers for them, parallel to the service in the men's hall. On occasion she even preached. At first, women were not required or expected to attend synagogue regularly (although they might come to hear the sermon). It was not until the fifteenth century that their presence became fully accepted and synagogues were designed from the outset with this in view. In Nuremberg women even had their own synagogue.

One of the earliest synagogues in Ashkenaz, of which a fragment has been preserved, stood in Speyer but only two windows in Romanesque style, dating from the late eleventh century,

Above left: Priestly blessing being given in a German synagogue, 1508. The congregation avert their eyes since it is traditionally forbidden to look at the priests during the blessing. Their eyes are veiled to indicate their blindness to Christianity. Woodcut from 'Libellus de Judaica Confessione sive Sabbate' by the apostate and anti-Jewish agitator, Johannes Pfefferkorn, 1508. (*Jewish National and University Library, Jerusalem*)

Above right: Interior of a synagogue during the blowing of the *shofar*. The ark hangs on the far wall and there is a shelf for candles along the northern and southern walls. The women's section, curtained off from the men, is in the foreground. Wooduct from 'Libellus de Judaica Corfessione sive Sabbate' by Johannes Pfefferkorn, 1508. (*Jewish National and University Library, Jerusalem*)

Opposite, above: Praying in the synagogue, South Germany, 1320. From left to right: the *hazzan*, a bearded Jew and a young man holding the festival prayer-book (*mahzor*). Both the latter have the hat which Jews were forced to wear. Illumination from the 'Leipzig Mahzor'. (*Leipzig, Universitätsbibliothek*)

Opposite, below: A *hazzan* at a reading desk, depicted with a bird's head to circumvent the rabbinical ban on portraying the human face. Illumination from the 'Birds' Head Haggada', South Germany, *c.*1300. (*Israel Museum, Jerusalem*)

Overleaf: Torah scrolls in an open ark. Illumination from a *mahzor* of the Ashkenazi rite, after 1460. (*Bayerische Staatsbibliothek, Munich*)

4

can still be seen in the local museum. The synagogue was first built in 1096 and a hundred years later, following a blood libel, it was destroyed. The local ruler ordered it to be rebuilt but the community, like others in Germany, continued its chequered history of expulsion and return, and traces of the synagogue disappeared. Today, at the end of Judenbadgasse ('Street of the Jewish Bath'), not far from the great cathedral of Speyer, there remains only the ancient underground ritual bath, close to the site of the synagogue, which was constructed in the fourteenth century. From the remains and descriptions, it has been surmised that the synagogue was a vaulted structure, with a small rounded apse at its eastern end, and a women's section.

Not far away, in the town of Worms, stands the most famous of the Rhineland synagogues, built in 1034 and reconstructed in the twelfth century. The reconstruction is commemorated by a long inscription relating to the building of Solomon's Temple. It was only in the twentieth century that a scholar working on this inscription discovered that the numerical value of the Hebrew letters equals 4935, the Hebrew year corresponding to 1174–5, thus providing an exact date for its rebuilding. (The famous Worms Cathedral was built in this period and scholars have discerned some similarities in architectural detail.) The synagogue was restored a second time in 1611 and a few years later an addition was made to provide housing for the rabbinical academy. It was called the Rashi Chapel after the famous French medieval Bible and Talmud commentator who had studied in Worms more than five centuries earlier. A stone chair built into the wall was piously believed to have been Rashi's chair. On 9 November 1938 the notorious 'Crystal Night', when the Nazis destroyed synagogues throughout Germany and Austria, the Worms Synagogue was also razed. After the war the West German government ordered its complete reconstruction. This was accomplished with the utmost accuracy and faithfulness and reopened in 1961. All that remains of the original

synagogue are some fragments, now displayed in the courtyard. In the grounds, narrow steps lead down to the subterranean ritual bath, constructed in the twelfth century – as in Speyer next to the synagogue. The synagogue stands in the old, narrow Jews' Street (Judengasse, now inhabited largely by workers from Turkey) and remains its outstanding landmark.

The Worms Synagogue was imitated in many communities throughout Ashkenaz. Two Romanesque columns down the centre of the rectangular (49 ft × 31 ft) prayer hall divide the building into two naves of equal size. (Some authorities suggest that two columns were employed to recall the two columns at the entrance to Solomon's Temple, but in fact they are copied from church architecture of the time.) The columns' carvings and decorations were made by a Jewish artist whose name was preserved in an inscription. The reader's platform is in the centre of the building, and his view of the ark is effectively blocked by one of the columns. Formerly, as shown by etchings of the mid-nineteenth century, the platform was enclosed by a large pseudo-Gothic structure. The women's chamber, built in 1213, is a large room at right angles to the prayer hall. The wall separating the women from the men was replaced by two large doors in the middle of the nineteenth century and then removed, so that there is now no division between the two rooms.

The origin of the twin-nave format has been disputed. Some say it derived from contemporary ecclesiastical or secular patterns (as in town halls or monastic dining rooms); others believe that it was based on Middle Eastern, especially Palestinian, models. In any case, it spread to synagogues across Europe between the twelfth and sixteenth centuries, through Germany, to Bohemia, and eventually to Poland. In Worms the entrance was in the east but elsewhere access was usually in the northern or southern wall so that the worshipper's attention was immediately attracted to the reader's platform, designed as the main focus. (This was changed

Left: Entrance to the subterranean ritual bath in the courtyard of the Worms Synagogue. Drawing by Erna Salzer, Worms, 1928.
(*Stadtliches Kulturinstitut, Worms*)

Below: Synagogue at Worms with the women's section in the left background. Photo taken before its destruction in 1938.
(*Stadtliches Kulturinstitut, Worms*)

Interior of the men's hall, Worms synagogue.
Lithograph by Abraham Heu, *c.*1840.
(*Stadtliches Kulturinstitut, Worms*)

Opposite: Exterior of the Rashi Chapel, Worms Synagogue.
(*Beth Hatefutsoth model/Photo: Michael Horton*)

Above: Interior of the Rashi Chapel, Worms Synagogue. Rashi, the famous French medieval scholar, studied for a time in Worms in the eleventh century and this addition to the building was constructed in 1624 and named in his memory. The so-called 'chair of Rashi' (at the back) is apocryphal. This chapel was in fact a study room, largely reconstructed in 1855.
(*Beth Hatefutsoth model/Photo: Michael Horton*)

in the sixteenth century when the authoritative legal code, the *Shulhan Aruch*, laid down that a Jew must enter the synagogue in the direction of prayer.) The main problem with the design was that pillars obscured the view of the ark for some of the congregation.

A twin-nave synagogue at Regensburg in Germany is known to us through sixteenth-century etchings made shortly before its destruction. (The etchings were made by a member of the Regensburg town council which decreed the expulsion of the Jews and the demolition of their house of worship.) Here there were three columns and the reader's platform was somewhat to the right of centre in order to ensure a view of the ark. The floor was sunken and the architecture provides a link between the Romanesque construction in Worms and the Gothic Altneuschul in Prague.

The building of twin-nave synagogues came to an end in Germany with the Crusades, when Jewish houses of worship were being destroyed and it seemed pointless to build new ones.

The Altneuschul ('Old-New Synagogue') is perhaps Europe's most famous synagogue and the oldest still in use. Most of it dates from the late fourteenth century and its exterior was unusually impressive for the Middle Ages. This was possible because it was hidden away in the heart of the Jewish quarter, well out of Christian sight. It is the most pronouncedly Gothic of all known synagogues. It reflected contemporary architecture in Prague, and was to influence subsequent examples in eastern

Opposite, far left: Exterior of the Regensburg Synagogue, built in the fourteenth century. Two pillars stand before the two-storeyed portico symbolic of those of Solomon's Temple.
(*Yad Vashem, Jerusalem*)

Opposite: Interior of the Regensburg Synagogue, drawn in 1519 by Albrecht Altdorfer, shortly before its destruction. The central row of pillars divides the hall into twin naves.
(*Kupferstichkabinett SMPK, Berlin*)

Right: The entrance to the Altneuschul, Prague. Etching by Jos. I. Hettich, nineteenth century.
(*Judaica Photo Archive, Israel Museum, Jerusalem*)

Below right: The wrought-iron reader's desk in the centre of the Altneuschul. Nineteenth-century etching.
(*Beth Hatefutsoth Archive, Tel Aviv*)

Below: The Altneuschul, Prague. Etching from a drawing by Wurbs, 1860.
(*Beth Hatefutsoth Archive, Tel Aviv*)

Above: The Altneuschul ('Old-New Synagogue'), Prague, so called because it was preceded by an 'Old Synagogue' and a 'New Synagogue'. The grey stone edifice, built *c.*1280 in the Jewish quarter of Prague, has inspired many legends, including one of a dove miraculously protecting the synagogue when it was threatened by fire.
(*Beth Hatefutsoth model/Photo: Michael Horton*)

Opposite: The gloomy Gothic interior of the Altneuschul, Prague, looking towards the reader's desk between the twin pillars and to the ark at the far end. The floor is below street level to provide the maximum internal height and still comply with external building restrictions on the height of synagogues. The reader's desk is a stone platform with a wrought-iron grille. The benches along the wall, originally of stone, are now covered with wood.
(*Beth Hatefutsoth model/Photo: Michael Horton*)

Europe. The hall is not large (49 ft × 29 ft), and is divided into two naves by two octagonal pillars. A stone platform originally stood near the ark, but in the late fifteenth century this was moved back to take up the space between the two pillars. As in Worms, the women were placed in a special building (along the western wall), connected to the prayer hall by windows three feet above the floor. In the main hall the narrow Gothic windows let in little light and the dim atmosphere conveyed a mystic impression which inspired many folk stories. According to Jewish legend it was here that the seventeenth-century rabbi, Judah Loew, created the *Golem*, a mechanical monster designed to rescue the Jews of Prague from oppression but who got out of control.

Another form of synagogue, which was popular in Germany in the Middle Ages, was an elongated structure with a single nave, as at Speyer. This type was contemporaneous with the double-nave synagogues and was considered more appropriate for smaller communities whose requirements were modest. The platform was constructed in the centre and the absence of pillars solved the problem of seeing the ark in its niche in the eastern wall. The women's section was often a gallery running the length of one of the walls (sometimes as an external annexe); where this was inadequate, a second storey was added for the women. (In Frankfurt the women had a separate three-storey building.) The single-nave form also spread from Germany (as in Fürth and Miltenberg, for example), to Bohemia (the Pinkas and Altschul synagogues in Prague) and to Poland (as in Poznan, for example).

The central role of the synagogue in the life of the Jews, as it crystallized during the Middle Ages, was to serve as a universal pattern until the advent of the Emancipation. The synagogue was the hub of communal life and the Jews wanted to live as close to it as possible. It became natural to observe the rabbinical command to hasten to the synagogue but to depart from it slowly and with regret. Congregants would vie with each other for the honour of keeping it clean. In Frankfurt women almost came to blows fighting for the privilege, and the honour was sometimes put up for sale, with the proceeds going to the upkeep of the building. There is even a report of a pious Rabbi Jacob who insisted on using his beard to sweep the area in front of the ark until the rabbinical authorities condemned such behaviour as showing lack of respect for the beard, which also had religious significance.

There was something going on at the synagogue at all hours of the day – and much of the night. Many worshippers attended the three daily services but the largest congregations were present on the Sabbath and festivals. (If the number of regular worshippers dropped for any reason, a certain number of Jews were paid to attend regularly and make up the prayer quorum. They were known as the *batlanim*, literally 'idlers'.) When the Jew attended synagogue, especially on the Sabbath and festivals, he donned a special coat, cap, and shoes (an iron scraper was provided at the entrance for him to clean his boots). Inside the prayer hall he felt completely relaxed and at home. The strict decorum of the Church was alien to him. With the exception of certain parts of the service which were treated with reverence (such as the eighteen benedictions), he would sing lustily (not always to the same tune as the reader), converse with his neighbour and, from time to time, walk around. He sincerely believed that he was conducting a dialogue with God, only his God was not some ineffable transcendent being; he was more like his neighbour.

Children were indulged – some would say overindulged – and were not only seen but often heard. On certain occasions they were featured in the ritual. On Friday evenings, for example, they sipped from the wine cup after the Sabbath benediction. On the Feast of the Rejoicing of the Law, they were called up *en masse* to a special reading from the Torah. And talented boys were called to read the prophetical portions of the week on the Sabbath, even before they had reached official maturity.

Top: Old (*right*) and new (*left*) synagogue in Fürth, near Nuremberg. The old masonry synagogue was built in 1615–16 and was requisitioned for some time as a jail and a stable. The new wooden synagogue was built in 1697. Engraving by Johann Alexander Boener, 1705. (*Jüdisches Lexikon, Berlin, 1928*)

Above: Interior of the Fürth Synagogue. The individual reading desks for the men are arranged across the hall and along the sides. One access to the two-storeyed grilled women's gallery was up the steps in the right-hand corner. Engraving by Johann Alexander Boener, 1705. (*Jüdisches Lexikon, Berlin, 1928*)

Of course, reasonable limits were imposed. Frivolity was not permitted, nor could commerce be conducted inside the prayer hall – although the raising of funds for communal purposes or charity was allowed. Funds for the synagogue were obtained from various sources: from auctioning the right to perform honoured rituals (such as dressing the Torah scroll or opening the ark); from the general community chest; from donations made by people called up to the Torah reading; and from contributions made when memorial prayers were recited.

Generally speaking, within the context of medieval society, the synagogue was a democratic institution. Every adult male was counted in the prayer quorum and could be called to the reading of the Torah and, if he knew how, could be asked to lead the prayer service. Perhaps the most remarkable expression of democracy was the right of any congregant to interrupt the service and demand redress of any injustice which he felt he had suffered. Prayers would be delayed until the complainant was satisfied that his grievance would be properly examined. Everyone had a say in community affairs. But although everyone was equal, some were 'more equal'. The scholar was accorded great deference and all rose from their seats in the synagogue whenever he appeared. Also, the more affluent had a disproportionate influence in the governance of the community and the synagogue, a privilege that

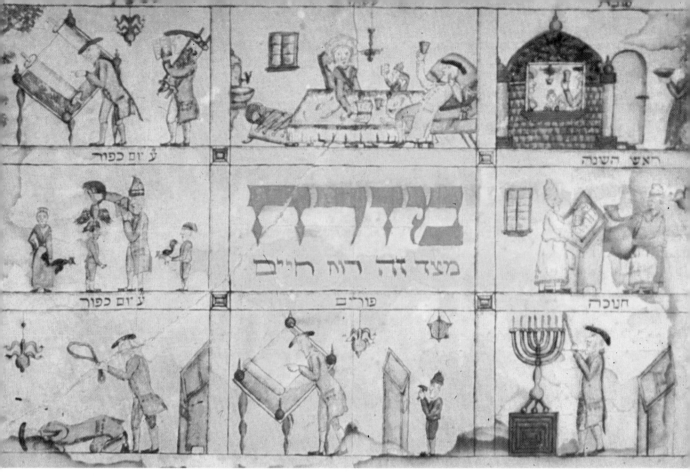

עָ יוֹם כִּפּוּר   ראש השנה

מצד זה רוח חיים

עָ יום כפור   פורי''ם   חנוכה

Opposite: New Year service in a Prague synagogue, possibly the Pinkas Synagogue. The *shofar* is sounded on the reader's platform (*centre*) in front of the opened ark. On the left is the two-storeyed women's section. Eighteenth-century woodcut.
(*From P.C.Kirchner's 'Jüdisches Ceremoniel', Nuremberg, 1734*)

Above: A *mizrah* (plaque placed on the eastern wall of the synagogue) from eighteenth-century Germany. Its folk depiction of festivals and customs shows (clockwise from top left-hand corner): *Shavuot*; Passover (the *seder*); Tabernacles; New Year; *Hanukka*; *Purim*; Day of Atonement, flagellation; Day of Atonement, expiation ceremony.
(*Feuchtwanger Collection, Israel Museum, Jerusalem*)

was passed down from father to son.

The synagogue was the natural venue for a great variety of activities. Solemn oaths were taken before the sacred ark, and the Torah scroll personified as a witness. Bans of excommunication on miscreants were issued and announcements of lost or stolen property were made in the holy environment. Weddings were held in the synagogue or, if possible, in the courtyard (the *schulhof*). It was there that the monthly blessing on the moon was pronounced and funeral orations delivered for community leaders. When weather permitted, the law court might sit in the courtyard and in some places (such as Frankfurt-on-Main in the fifteenth century) the Jews held their market there. On weekdays worshippers would bring their breakfast and consume it in the courtyard before going to work since the law prohibited them from eating before prayers. Wedding feasts and other festive meals connected with the observance of the Commandments could be held in the prayer hall.

The synagogue was used also for secular purposes, notably community meetings, and if there was no suitable annexe, classes would be held there. Other community facilities would often be found in the synagogue complex – the community offices, the courtroom, the ritual bath, the storeroom for damaged or worn scrolls and books, the library (especially after the advent of printing), a hospice for travellers from other communities, a social hall (known in Germany as 'the dance house'), living

21.Kupf. Die Hochzeit Procession.

Reumonds Gebeth auſer dem Tempel.

Above: Monthly ceremony of blessing the moon, outside the Fürth Synagogues (*background right*).
(*From P.C.Kirchner's 'Jüdisches Ceremoniel',
Nuremberg, 1734*)

Opposite above: Wedding ceremony in the courtyard of the Fürth Synagogue.
(*From P.C.Kirchner's 'Jüdisches Ceremoniel',
Nuremberg, 1734*)

Opposite, below: Wedding procession in the courtyard of the Fürth Synagogue.
(*From P.C.Kirchner's 'Jüdisches Ceremoniel',
Nuremberg, 1734*)

quarters for the sexton and his family, and even prison cells.

The synagogue and its study room were the centre of the Jew's religious and cultural life. Together with the home, they constituted the poles of his Judaism, of his very existence, and he would spend as much time in the synagogue as at home. After all, the rabbis threatened: 'He who does not go to the synagogue in this world will not be allowed to go in the next world.'

SPAIN AND PORTUGAL

WHAT does the Church of Corpus Christi in Segovia have in common with the Chapel of the Dormition of the Virgin in Toledo, and the Church of St Bartholomew in Seville? The answer is that originally they were all synagogues, and their fate mirrors the tragedy that befell the Jews of Spain in the Middle Ages.

When the country was under Moslem rule, its Jews flourished and their so-called 'Golden Age' was one of the outstanding 'success stories' of pre-Emancipation Jewish history. Their cultural and religious creativity found expression in some of the great classics of Jewish literature. Their status and affluence doubtless also found expression in their religious buildings, but none has survived the Moslem era.

After the Christian conquest the Jews at first continued to thrive and to receive marks of favour. For example, in Seville in 1248 the ruler, who was interested in repopulating the city, presented the Jews with three former mosques to convert into synagogues. Almost 120 synagogues are known to have existed in Christian Spain. Every community had at least one and some had many more: the affluent community of Seville had twenty-three; Toledo, with fifteen thousand Jews, had nine famous synagogues; and Valladolid is known to have lost eight synagogues during one war. In the Jewish quarter of Calatayud, so many Jews prayed in private synagogues that the seven main synagogues suffered from a sparsity of attendance. Jewish guilds and fraternities constructed their own places of worship. The weavers' guild and the benevolent society, for example, each had their own synagogue in Calatayud, while in Huesca the Jewish burial society had its own. All the building was

Opposite: Reader in a Spanish synagogue reciting the Passover Haggada from his platform to members of the community unable to read the book in their own homes. The synagogue is adorned with hanging Moorish lamps and a high platform on columns. From the fourteenth-century illuminated manuscript known as 'Sister' to the Golden Haggada.
(*British Library, London*)

Right: Worshippers in a Spanish synagogue. The reader holds the Torah scroll as the congregation stands respectfully. Illustration to Psalm 113 in the fourteenth-century Barcelona Haggada.
(*British Library, London*)

funded by voluntary contributions or by individual philanthropists and there was seldom any need for a community tax for synagogues. The privilege of establishing synagogues was encouraged by Spain's rulers who conferred it upon their Jewish courtiers as a personal favour. James I of Aragon gave permission to one of his Jewish subjects 'to build a synagogue in his own home or anywhere else in the Barcelona Jewish quarter'. The code of Alfonso X of Castile expressly outlawed breaking into or robbing a synagogue, 'for a synagogue is a house where the name of God is praised'.

The main synagogues were located in the heart of the Jewish quarter both for the convenience of the worshippers and to ensure easy access in times of danger. They were the most important buildings in the quarter and although care was taken not to overshadow any nearby churches, they dominated their surroundings. The main synagogue in Cordova was of such magnificence and height that Pope Innocent IV issued a bull enjoining the Christians of the town to stop its building 'as it would cause a scandal among the faithful and harm the Church of Cordova'.

As in Ashkenaz, the synagogues in Spain served many purposes. Here the law courts sat, royal decrees were read out to the congregation, lost articles announced, and oaths administered. Entrance was often through an open courtyard, which was a favourite meeting place as well as the scene of many of the community's administrative activities. Communal buildings such as the assembly hall, the school, the offices, the social centre, and the hostel, were often located on either side of the synagogue.

Tragedy struck Spanish Jewry at the end of the fourteenth century with a wave of massacres, forced conversion, and the savage destruction of synagogues (on a scale presaging the notorious *Kristallnacht* in Nazi Germany). From then on the situation of the Jews deteriorated rapidly. Many synagogues that were spared destruction were turned into churches in the spirit of one of the Popes who had

Reader and congregation reciting the *Hallel* prayer. The reader, dressed in white, is on a high platform reached by stairs. Illustration from the fourteenth-century Spanish manuscript, the Kaufmann Haggada.
(*Academy of Sciences, Budapest*)

ordered that 'places divested of the blind Jewish perversion of faith should receive the light of grace under the name of Christianity'. It was at this period that the Jews were forced to listen to conversionist sermons and, on the orders of the Dominicans, had to assemble regularly in the synagogues to hear the preaching of the friars urging them to adopt Christianity.

When the persecutions abated, some of the buildings were restored to the Jews. New synagogues were constructed but they were kept on a modest scale and carefully restricted

Interior of a Spanish synagogue, through an arched door. The Torah scrolls stand in the ark, their silk covers embroidered with silver and gold, and adorned with silver crowns. Two glass lamps hang in front of the ark. The wooden reading table on columns occupies a considerable area. The congregants are leaving at the end of the service. From the fourteenth-century Sarajevo Haggada.
(*National Museum, Sarajevo*)

tians Gothic influences intruded. In the interiors, Moorish arches and impressive octagonal columns with carved capitals were among the notable features. Some synagogues had carved stone benches along the walls for the congregants, whose children sat at their feet (when they sat at all). Others had benches, chairs or even divans, and the worshippers were often responsible for providing their own seating. As in Ashkenaz, seat ownership was officially recorded and was transferable by gift, sale, or bequest. Those who could not afford to purchase a seat rented one. On one occasion in Calatayud the king himself turned to the Jewish community to obtain the privilege of constructing two seats for his jeweller. The women seem to have been seated in special galleries. The interior was illuminated by various types of brass or bronze lamps, some in a Moorish style, some star-shaped. On the eves of the Sabbath and festivals, hundreds of candles glittered in the synagogue hall.

Direct knowledge of the appearance of these synagogues comes from two main sources: illuminated manuscripts of the time and the few extant synagogues, all from the Christian period (whose chance preservation stems from their having been turned into churches). Not only the architecture but also the decorations reveal a strong Moorish influence. First of all there are the adornments in the form of geometric patterns. Then there are the long panels incorporating verses from the Bible which are written in elegant characters inspired by Arabic calligraphy, and recall the similar application of verses from the Koran, found in mosques.

The Spanish architects made their own contribution to the problem of the tension between the ark and the reader's platform in the prayer hall. Judging from manuscript illustrations, the platform was, at first, of minor importance – a light timber construction at the western side of the hall. Then the platform was attached to the western wall. The resultant 'double focus' of ark and platform was to inspire synagogue design in other lands. The

by the clergy. But this proved to be only an interlude. In 1415, a papal bull stipulated that all newly-built or repaired synagogues should be closed. Only one synagogue, the very smallest, would be allowed to remain in each quarter, regardless of the size of the community. In 1492 the end came with the general expulsion of the Jews from Spain. All synagogues then in existence were confiscated and taken over by the Royal Treasury and many were converted into churches.

The predominant design of the Spanish synagogues was Moorish but under the Chris-

Above: Interior of the thirteenth-century Santa Maria La Blanca Synagogue, Toledo. Four long arcades of horseshoe arches divide the interior into five bays. The capitals of the pillars are richly carved and the bases decorated with glazed tiles.
(*Beth Hatefutsoth model/Photo: Michael Horton*)

Opposite: Exterior of Santa Maria La Blanca, Toledo. The simple brick exterior does not prepare the visitor for the grandeur of the interior.
(*Beth Hatefutsoth model/Photo: Michael Horton*)

platform itself was elevated on columns to a considerable height with access up a flight of steps, reminiscent of pulpits in mosques and churches. Around one side ran a ledge on which the Torah scroll could be placed while being read. The double-doored ark was in a niche above floor level and the scrolls were kept inside in a standing position.

Four noteworthy buildings have survived, two in Toledo, one in Cordova and one in Segovia. The earliest is the Toledo Synagogue built about 1200 and now known as Santa María La Blanca (Saint Mary the White, the name of the convent for repentant fallen women into which it was converted in the sixteenth century). It had been confiscated from the Jews and turned into a church in the early fifteenth century, following an attack on it by a mob during the anti-Jewish outbreaks of that period. The convent was succeeded by a church and then, for some time during the late eighteenth century, it was used as an armoury. In the mid-nineteenth century it was declared a national monument and restored. Of modest exterior, it has a striking Moorish-inspired interior with four arcades of octagonal pillars, thirty-two in number, supporting horseshoe-shaped arches. Its area (85 ft × 62 ft) is comparatively small, but the placement of the arches and columns gives an impression of

Below: Interior of Santa María La Blanca, Toledo. Twenty-four octagonal brick piers separate the five aisles and support twenty-eight horseshoe arches. Another eight half-piers are attached to the walls. Nineteenth-century lithograph.
(*Jewish National and University Library, Jerusalem*)

Opposite: Interior of the Cordova Synagogue showing the niche in the western wall.
(*Courtesy of David Davidovitch, Tel Aviv*)

spaciousness. The capitals of the pillars are decorated with pine-cones, a familiar theme in Spanish design of that time. The small windows in the western wall probably led to a women's section, but this is no longer in existence.

The Cordova Synagogue was built in 1315 and taken over by the state in 1492. It was first used as a hospital for rabies patients, then as a church belonging to the guild of shoemakers and dedicated to St Crispin and St Crispinian. Towards the end of the nineteenth century it was declared a national monument and restored to its original design. Entrance is through a forecourt into the small (21 ft × 23 ft) hall, above which a gallery for women was added. A niche in the eastern wall held the ark while the platform apparently adjoined the western wall. Most of the original decoration disappeared in the course of time but the wall retains ornamentation in the form of Hebrew verses from the Psalms. The unwavering belief of the Jews in their eventual return to Zion is vividly illustrated by the inscription on the western wall, declaring that the building is only to be regarded as a 'temporary structure', and adding: 'Arise, O Lord, and hasten to rebuild Jerusalem.' The western wall has a dedication in Arabic, the only one found in a Spanish synagogue.

The second fine synagogue in Toledo dates from 1357. After the expulsion of the Jews it became first a priory belonging to the Calatravan Order of Knights, and later the Chapel of the Dormition of the Virgin, known in Spanish as the Érmita del Tránsito de Nuestra Señora. This explains its usual name

Opposite: The Cordova Synagogue looking towards the entrance. The vestibule and gallery were later additions to the building.
(Courtesy of David Davidovitch, Tel Aviv)

Above: Interior wall of the 'El Transito' Synagogue, Toledo, showing the ornamental plasterwork and the three rows of Biblical inscriptions in Hebrew along the top of the walls (above, under the arches, and bottom).
(Beth Hatefutsoth model/Photo: Michael Horton)

today, the El Tránsito Synagogue, now also a national monument. From the florid inscriptions on the wall we know the identity of the original patron (Samuel Halevi Abulafia) and architect (Meir Abdeli). Abulafia was treasurer of King Pedro the Cruel of Castile, and helped the monarchy by improving the king's finances. In 1360, however, the king ordered his arrest, confiscated his large fortune, and sent him to Seville, where he was tortured to death. It is somewhat ironic now to read a dedication to King Pedro on the synagogue wall. Abulafia's home stood next to the synagogue, and was probably even joined to it. A nearby building was later the home of El Greco and today houses an El Greco Museum.

From the outside the building is not impressive but it has maintained its original inner grandeur. It has a single-nave hall (75 ft × 31 ft). Workmen were brought from Granada to build and decorate it and their exquisite workmanship can be discerned, for

example, in the capitals of the fifty-four pillars. The gallery, with loggias, presumably for the women congregants, is under a cedar ceiling (the cedar, according to tradition, was brought especially from Lebanon). The floor was originally a mosaic, of which only a small fragment has been preserved. Today the hall contains nineteen graves of knights of the Calatravan Order, buried here in the sixteenth century. Most striking are the rich decorations on the walls with their colourful stucco ornamentation of floral and geometric motifs and three parallel bands of Hebrew verse from the Bible. The alabaster slabs which screen off the women's section are ornamented with the biblical Song of Miriam. There are dedicatory panels on either side of the ark niche, one of which reads: 'The house which Samuel [Abulafia] built, with a wooden tower [i.e. the tall platform for the reader] for the Reading of the Torah and its Torah scrolls, with their crowns, and its bowls for washing and lamps for

Left: An imagined reconstruction of El Tránsito as a synagogue. Etching by I. J. Rawlins, 1848.
(*From E. H. Lindo's 'The History of the Jews in Spain and Portugal'*, London, 1848)

Opposite, above: Exterior of the mid-fourteenth-century El Tránsito Synagogue, Toledo, built of brick and stone. The belfry was added when the building was used by Christians.
(*Keter Publishing House, Jerusalem*)

Opposite, below: Interior of the El Tránsito Synagogue looking towards the site of the ark, formerly located in the triple arch. When the building was transferred to the Knights of the Order of the Calatrava after the Jews were expelled from Spain, members of the Order were buried in the hall and some of their graves are in the centre. The two windows high in the eastern wall may portray or symbolize the tablets of the law.
(*Beth Hatefutsoth Archive, Tel Aviv*)

lighting, and windows like the windows of Ariel [i.e. Jerusalem].' The shape of the two windows high on the eastern wall has given rise to the speculation that they may originally have been depictions of the two tablets of the law.

The fourth extant Spanish synagogue from the end of the fourteenth century is in Segovia. In 1410 it was turned into the Corpus Christi Church. It bears a striking resemblance to the La Blanca Synagogue, originally having the same octagonal columns, horseshoe arches, and pine-cone motifs on the capitals.

A recent discovery has been the old synagogue in Gerona under a site still known as the 'Square of the Rabbis'. The entrance to the synagogue and the ritual bath have been excavated and the prayer hall is in the process of being cleared. In one of the walls, the opening of a stove for baking unleavened bread (*matza*) was discovered. In it was a fragment of unleavened bread; but as soon as it was exposed to the air, this *matza*, preserved for almost five hundred years, turned to dust.

Jews also lived in Portugal in the Middle Ages and the community there suffered a similar fate to that of the Jews in Spain. The synagogue of Tomar, north-east of Lisbon, is the oldest synagogue in Portugal in a state of good preservation. It was built between 1430 and 1460 and was only in use until 1496 when the ruler ordered all Jews to convert to Christianity or leave the country. In 1516 the building was turned into a prison with the window at the top of one of the walls used by the warders to watch the prisoners below. In 1600 it was converted into a Catholic chapel and later into a grocery warehouse. In 1923 Samuel Schwartz, a Jewish mining engineer from Poland who devoted himself to the study of Portuguese Jewry, bought the building, had it restored, and donated it to the Portuguese nation on condition that it be used to house a Portuguese Jewish museum. The Synagogue was a small (31ft × 27ft) square building, to which a women's annexe was later added on its eastern side.

Top: Entrance to the Isaac el Cec Synagogue in Gerona. The interior is at present being excavated. (*Photo: Rosemarie Trostel*)

Above: Original door to the Tomar Synagogue, today a Jewish museum. (*From J.M.Santos Simones, 'Tomar e a sua Juderia', Tomar, 1943*)

Interior of the Corpus Christi Church in Segovia, which was a synagogue until 1410, and was restored in 1899 after severe fire damage. (*Courtesy of David Davidovitch, Tel Aviv*)

Above: Entrance to a building in Castelo de Vide, Portugal, thought to have been a synagogue. (*Beth Hatefutsoth Archive, Tel Aviv/Photo: Frederic Brenner*)

Below: Inside the Tomar Synagogue, Portugal. (*Luso-Hebraico Museum, Tomar*)

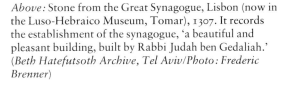

Above: Stone from the Great Synagogue, Lisbon (now in the Luso-Hebraico Museum, Tomar), 1307. It records the establishment of the synagogue, 'a beautiful and pleasant building, built by Rabbi Judah ben Gedaliah.'
(*Beth Hatefutsoth Archive, Tel Aviv/Photo: Frederic Brenner*)

Below: The hall of the presumed ex-synagogue in Castelo de Vide.
(*Beth Hatefutsoth Archive, Tel Aviv/Photo: Frederic Brenner*)

Above: Stone with inscription from an ancient synagogue at Belmonte, Portugal (thirteenth century), now in the Luso-Hebraico Museum, Tomar. It reads: 'God is in His sacred temple; all the earth becomes silent before Him.' Earlier this century it was discovered that a considerable part of the population of Belmonte was descended from Marranos who continued to observe Jewish customs.
(*Beth Hatefutsoth Archive, Tel Aviv/Photo: Frederic Brenner*)

5

RENAISSANCE AND GHETTO

IN 1486 the distinguished Italian scholar Obadiah of Bertinoro visited Palermo in Sicily. Its 850 Jewish families all resided on a single street in the best part of the town. Obadiah was deeply impressed with the synagogue, and he described it in detail in his travel diary:

There is no synagogue in the world that compares with the one in Palermo. In its courtyard the grapevines entwine the stone pillars. I have never seen such vines – five spans thick. Stone steps lead down to another courtyard which stands before the synagogue. This has a porch on three sides with large chairs for those who do not want to go into the synagogue and also a magnificent well.

The synagogue is forty cubits square. On the eastern side stands the ark, a domed stone structure. The scrolls are not kept in a chest as is our custom but laid on a wooden shelf. They are ornamented with crowns and finials of silver and precious stones, valued by the local Jews at 4,000 pieces of gold. The ark has two doors and two members of the congregation are entrusted with opening and closing them. A wooden tower in the centre serves as the reader's platform. The community employs five readers and on Sabbaths and festivals they chant the prayers in the sweetest voices I ever heard. But on weekdays so few come to service that a child could count them.

He goes on to enumerate the community buildings that surround the synagogue, including a magnificent mansion used as offices and as a lawcourt. One of the unusual customs that struck him was that, in general, coffins were taken into the synagogue vestibule for funeral services, while for especially learned congregants the coffin was brought inside the synagogue and a scroll of the law was removed from the ark while the funeral service was recited. On the eve of the Day of Atonement and on Hoshana Rabba, officials opened the ark and remained there all night; the women of the community would come in family groups to prostrate themselves and kiss the scrolls.

Obadiah's description is of particular interest because of the paucity of information on synagogues in Italy prior to the sixteenth century. In the Middle Ages Italian Jews were to be found almost entirely in southern Italy, Sicily and Sardinia. When the Jews left or were expelled, some of their synagogues were destroyed while others became churches. Some churches existing today are known to have originally been synagogues: the best-known examples are at Trani, near Bari, at Trapani in Sicily, and Cagliari in Sardinia. Trani, it is known, had three synagogues; the section of one of the two preserved, dating from 1247, is a domed covered hall that from the exterior looks like a hexagonal tower. No synagogues have survived in central or northern Italy from before the sixteenth century.

Italian Jewry as a whole was constituted by various Jewish communities, each with their own liturgical rites, traditions, and melodies.

Jew holding a Torah scroll, from the 'Jerusalem Mishneh Torah', c.1400
(*Jewish National and University Library, Jerusalem*)

וראזחזור ומ שמר ונשמט מטה האחר וקו
וכל רב מת פטורו בכ שי אזמ דצ אנ וא ת
כן שאל־ רבכ ובכ לי ם ו מבי גו יד שבח ו
דצ אז וות והו ע ומן הק רי אה ו זן מ לון
יש למ טה צ זיר כ ב ה ן מון נ ישאי המ ט
אחד ואחד ל פי כח ו אם הי ה ודר אה ל י־ על יד ה טוב ה
ואם הי ה עד ל שפ תן מור כ פי יל ד
וכ ב כן התפלל כ ל אחד ואחד כ פי ב
פ עם אחת ב זים ו יש שב יתפלל פ ע מי
הז י ע סוק ן ב ה ספר והני ע ומן ק ש ו ־
ו בחד ומ ומת תמי ד ל פנ יהם כ ל הי מם ק וי
אין הכת ב כטל ל פנ יהם כ ל הימ ק ור
וב רוומ ש אין ה חזר בכ אר צית ה תני נ פרס
ו ילד ו להם בנ ים ב אר צית ה תני ם ו את
וש פתמ ס ו ית ה ש פ ת ב לאר י אחד ו אחד כ
ה וכ ה ו בון שה יה מ ד כ זר אינו מ טל ל

The original community, as already noted, came to Italy in the first century BC and until the early Middle Ages was concentrated almost entirely in the south. From the late thirteenth century it began to expand northward throughout the peninsula. The descendants of the original community were known as the 'Italiani'. In the fifteenth century they were joined by Ashkenazi Jews who, moving south from France and Germany, established their own communities and rabbinical academies. After the expulsions from Spain (1492) and Portugal (1496), Jewish refugees arrived from these countries and organized their own congregations side by side with those already existing, while in some places, such as Leghorn, they founded new communities. A further element consisted of Jews from the Middle East (including Jews from Spain and Portugal who had settled in the Balkans and Asia Minor and moved from there to Italy where they set up

Above left: Worshipper in a prayer shawl in front of a closed ark, from the 'Jerusalem Mishneh Torah', manuscript illuminated in Perugia, *c.*1400.
(*Jewish National and University Library, Jerusalem*)

Left: Worshipper kneeling before the reader's platform, Ferrara (?), from the Rothchild Miscellany, *c.*1470.
(*Israel Museum, Jerusalem*)

Opposite: Interior of Mantua Synagogue, 1435. The Torah scroll is about to be returned to the ark after the reading; the reader stands at his desk in the centre of the hall. The worshippers all wear prayer-shawls; the animals in the four corners illustrate the maxim 'Be strong as a leopard, light as an eagle, fleet as a hart, and strong as a lion to perform the will of thy Father who is in heaven.' (*Ethics of the Fathers,* 5:23). From an illuminated manuscript of 'Arbaah Turim' by Jacob Ben Asher.
(*Biblioteca Apostolica, the Vatican*)

their own congregations) known as the 'Levantines', notably in Venice and Ancona. Each group had, in addition to its special liturgical customs, its own synagogal traditions, and these were reflected in the houses of worship they built, often in close proximity to one another. At the same time all fell under the spell of their Italian surroundings and of the Renaissance, as could be seen in the synagogue interiors and in the design of ritual objects.

The Italian synagogues were generally modest structures, undistinguished from the outside. Many were not separate buildings but occupied the top floor or floors of multistoreyed buildings whose lower storeys were used for community offices, schoolrooms and apartments for the clergy. But inside they were an artistic treat. Particular attention was paid to the ark, the pulpit and their surroundings. Arcades and lattice-work set off the women's section. The walls were covered with precious

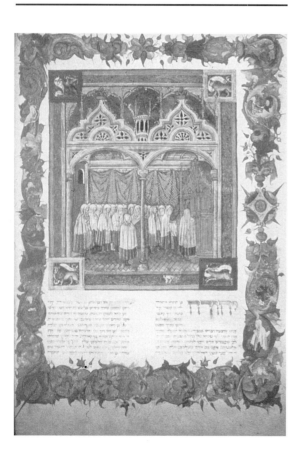

wood and, like the ceilings, elegantly ornamented, although representational art was eschewed. The overall impression was of tasteful harmony.

From the sixteenth century the bipolar pattern became the prevailing design: the ark constituted part of the eastern wall and the reader's platform, right at the other end, was attached to or constituted part of the western wall. The congregation sat facing each other on benches parallel to the northern and southern walls, leaving a large, spacious area in the centre. This space was used during special parts of the service, notably for the procession of worshippers carrying the Scroll of the Law from the ark to the reader's platform and back again. Services in the 'Italian' rite consisted largely of a 'dialogue' between the reader and the congregation, and the architecture of the hall was designed to meet this requirement. The seating arrangement also enabled the congregants to turn naturally towards either focus – the ark or the platform.

The platform was sometimes raised very high and in synagogues in Ancona and Pesaro, for example, it was almost a storey above the hall, resting on columns and attached to the wall. Access was from either side by an aesthetically-designed double staircase. In such cases the entrance to the synagogue hall was beneath the platform.

The rapid proliferation of synagogues during the Middle Ages angered the Church and in 1434 a bull was issued by Pope Eugenius IV forbidding the building of new synagogues. The papal bull was initially directed at Spain but was later extended to include Italy. Its effect, however, was short-lived. By the early sixteenth century in Rome, for example, in addition to six long-established Italian congregations and those of immigrants from France and Germany, new synagogues had been built by refugees, each according to their own tradition, among them Castilian, Catalan and Aragonese, and Sicilian. Before long they were joined by congregations of Jews emanating from Portugal, Provence, Naples, and

Opposite: Exterior of the Dubrovnik Synagogue,
Yugoslavia.
(*Beth Hatefutsoth model/Photo: Michael Horton*)

Above: Dubrovnik Synagogue. A Jewish community had
existed here since the fourteenth century, but its
character was changed with the arrival of refugees from
Spain and Portugal at the end of the fifteenth century.
Under Venetian rule, a street was allotted to the Jews
and its gate was closed at night. The synagogue was built
in its present form in the seventeenth century on the
second storey of a narrow ancient building. The
architecture was that of a typically small Sephardi
synagogue. The Torah scrolls (which were successfully
hidden from the Germans in the Second World War)
were presumably brought from Spain in 1492.
(*Beth Hatefutsoth model/Photo: Michael Horton*)

Opposite, above: Sounding the *shofar* (ram's horn) in a synagogue in northern Italy, from a north Italian *Mahzor* (festival prayer-book), 1460–70.
(*Courtesy of G. Weill, Jerusalem*)

Opposite, below: Praying in a synagogue in northern Italy. Each congregant has a desk, lit by a candle. The reader's desk is in front of the ark. From an Italian *Mahzor*, 1460–70.
(*Courtesy of G. Weill, Jerusalem*)

Above: Raised reader's desk in the Spanish synagogue, Pesaro, built in the second half of the sixteenth century and renovated in the eighteenth. The entrance to the prayer hall can be seen below the platform.
(*Judaica Photo Archive, Israel Museum, Jerusalem*)

The square of the New Ghetto in Venice. The Ashkenazi Synagogue is on the right, distinguished by the size of its upper windows.
(*Beth Hatefutsoth Archive, Tel Aviv/Photo: Micha Bar - Am*)

Tripoli. A similar proliferation occurred in cities in northern Italy.

With the advent of Protestantism the Jews were suspected by the Catholic Church of having helped to foment the Reformation. As a result, they became the prime target of the counter-Reformation, and were consigned to the fringes of society, to be isolated from the local population. The process began in Venice in 1516 when the Jews were ordered to live on a small island on the outskirts of the city, popularly called 'Ghetto'. From there the name spread and acquired a general usage. When in 1555 Pope Paul IV issued a bull decreeing the general seclusion of the Jews in all papal territories, the word 'ghetto' was understood by all. During the following two centuries Jewish communities in small towns and villages, as well as in some of the larger cities such as Bologna, were disbanded and the refugees went to live in the few cities where closed ghettos existed. At this time thirty thousand Jews lived in these ghettos under difficult physical and economic conditions, yet they faithfully preserved and developed their religious, cultural, and social traditions. The only urban centre in which Jews were not enclosed in a ghetto and could live where they chose was Leghorn (Livorno), the greatest centre of Spanish and Portuguese Jews in Italy.

The 1555 bull had decreed that each ghetto could have only one synagogue; all others were to be demolished and no new ones constructed. Thus 115 synagogues were closed down in the Papal States and the Jews in the remaining communities of Rome and Ancona had to pay a special tax for every synagogue closed. Bulls issued in the later sixteenth century and cancelled only in 1847 decreed that every week a certain number of Jews had to attend services conducted by a priest, preferably on the Jewish Sabbath; the conversionist sermon on this occasion was given, when possible, in Hebrew.

Segregation in the ghettos was not total. During the day the Jews could move outside and they were allowed to receive Christians who came to visit them. Christians were often attracted to the synagogues because of their beautiful baroque or rococo interiors. Indeed, some had been designed by the great Christian architects of the day and contained magnificent ceremonial objects, many of them also produced by non-Jewish craftsmen. But the exquisite curtains for the ark were embroidered by the women of the congregation. Music for the synagogue service was the work of Jewish composers, some of whose works are played to this day. The synagogues, on special occasions, were even used for concerts and theatrical performances which also attracted non-Jewish visitors.

The most famous group of ghetto synagogues, still extant, was in Venice. There is a document from 1515, which reports the Venetian city council's discussion of the proposed ghettoization and refers to the existence, at that time, of synagogues in various parts of the city. One advocate of segregation states that 'it is necessary for the peace of the city since Christian preachers ascribe the misfortunes that have visited the country to the excessive liberty

only giveaway is the large size of the windows). They were all approached by modest staircases leading to interiors that were masterpieces in their design, furnishing and decoration. The basic plan for all was a rectangular hall with the longer sides running from east to west, along which were rows of benches, leaving the centre of the hall free. The ark and seats of honour were in the east; the reading desk was raised on a high platform in the west with access by stairways. Below the ceiling was a latticed gallery for the women. The internal pillars were of marble while the walls were marble-faced, covered with gilded reliefs and wood carvings. The skilled craftsmanship of the furnishings was among the finest to be found in Italy at the time.

The oldest of the five main Venice synagogues is the fourth-floor Great Ashkenazi Synagogue, built in 1528–9, and renovated on a number of occasions, most thoroughly in 1733. Its main staircase, narrow and steep, ascends from a former anchorage for gondolas. (Pressure of space in the ghettos eventually necessitated the conversion of such 'docks' into additional housing areas.) Within, the ark and other ornaments are covered with gold leaf and this, together with the curtains and window hangings, formerly scarlet but now beige, conveys a warm, luxurious effect. Unusual for Italian synagogues is the long cursive inscription along and under the women's gallery containing the Ten Commandments. There are indications that, following Ashkenazi custom, the platform stood first in the centre of the hall but later, bowing to Italian usage, was pushed back to the western wall. The elliptical women's gallery was not part of the original construction but was added later, based on the design of the Spanish Synagogue.

The second Venetian synagogue, the Canton Synagogue, was also Ashkenazi. It is another architectural jewel and the first of the Venetian houses of worship to introduce the ark-platform bipolarity.

The most famous of all was the Spanish Synagogue, which has remained in regular use

granted to the Jews and to the existence of their synagogues'. No traces remain of these pre-ghetto synagogues. The decree establishing the ghetto forbade the building of synagogues but this was circumvented: the Jews succeeded in putting up at least nine synagogues, five of which became widely known and admired. The area of the ghetto was already built up when the Jews arrived and the only space for synagogues was on top of existing buildings, which proved an excellent way of keeping them concealed from the authorities. Moreover, by establishing them above the top floors of the buildings in which they were situated (the lower storeys usually housed communal institutions and non-Jewish families), they could observe the rabbinical precept concerning the desirability of making synagogues higher than their surroundings. In the Venice synagogues the floors were divided into two storeys, and the synagogues usually occupied the third and fourth floors.

The Venice synagogues are all virtually unrecognizable as such from the outside (the

Opposite: Exterior of the Great Ashkenazi Synagogue (Scuola Grande Tedesca) in Venice, founded in 1528–9. To avoid attention and to cope with crowded conditions, the main synagogues in the Venice ghetto were built on the upper storeys of existing buildings. From the outside they could be identified only by their enlarged windows.
(Beth Hatefutsoth model/Photo: Michael Horton)

Above: Interior of the Great Ashkenazi Synagogue, Venice, looking towards the ark. Four stone steps led to the ark, whose doors were decorated with amphorae. On either side are chairs for community leaders.
(Beth Hatefutsoth model/Photo: Michael Horton)

Above: Interior of the Canon Synagogue, Venice, an Ashkenazi synagogue founded in 1531 and renovated in 1736 and 1859. The ark is flanked by niches.
(*Judaica Photo Archive, Israel Museum, Jerusalem*)

Right: The ark in the Spanish synagogue, Venice, built in the sixteenth century and extensively remodelled in the seventeenth, probably by Longhena, the most eminent Venetian architect of his day. The doors of the ark date from 1755, but the ark itself may be earlier. The four columns may derive from the Arco Trionfale in Rome. Over the ark are the tablets of the law.
(*Beth Hatefutsoth Archive, Tel Aviv/Photo: Paolo Lombroso*)

Opposite: The Spanish Synagogue, Venice, looking towards the reader's platform, in the western wall (now a framework for the organ). Its scrolled canopy rested on four Corinthian columns. When the organ was installed in the nineteenth century, the reader's desk was moved close to the ark.
(*Judaica Photo Archive, Israel Museum, Jerusalem*)

to this day (the others have been closed for services for many years but are being renovated and reopened as museums). The largest of the five (65 ft × 40 ft), it was first constructed on a lower floor in the latter part of the sixteenth century. It was extensively remodelled on its present floor in 1655, probably by Baldassare Longhena, the best-known Venetian architect of his day (builder of the famous Venetian Church of Santa Maria Della Salute) or by one of his pupils. (A letter from the Venetian Jewish community to the Holy Land in 1655 expressed regret that they could not remit their usual contribution as they needed all their money for the synagogue construction.) Various elements in the synagogue interior correspond with

Longhena's other work. It has a strong gold and red motif and striking baroque decorations. The oval women's gallery (introduced in 1655) runs round the entire hall.

The synagogue of the Levantines dates from about the same time as the Sephardi Synagogue. Its twisted columns at each side of the reader's platform were a common feature in Italian synagogues; they were an imitation of Bernini's columns in St Peter's Cathedral, a Catholic interpretation of the columns in front of Solomon's Temple. The Italian Synagogue, more unassuming than the others, is closest to its original construction. Of the other small, private synagogues, two exist in the basements of the Levantine and Sephardi Synagogues.

Pre-ghetto Rome had at least fourteen synagogues, but when the Jews were herded into the ghetto only one was permitted. Providing

for differences among the various rites and communities was a problem, but an original solution was found. The five main synagogues (originally six) were housed in a single building and considered separate rooms of the same prayer house. This was accepted by the papal authorities. The site of a former church that had been deconsecrated became a two-wing structure to house the various prayer halls. One wing incorporated the Castilian Synagogue on its ground floor and the Italian-rite 'Temple' Synagogue one storey up. The 'Temple' Synagogue was Rome's senior, largest, and most prestigious congregation and enjoyed what was considered to be the choice location of the five. Its area was 65 ft × 40 ft, and a luxurious impression was created by the long hall, the four-columned portico in front of the ark, the high reader's desk on four pillars, and an elegant carved frieze depicting the Temple in Jerusalem. Above the ark was a depiction of the seven-branched candelabrum, based on the relief on Rome's Arch of Titus.

The second wing contained the Catalan-Aragonese Synagogue at the back, the Sicilian Synagogue on the first floor, and a second Italian-rite synagogue for Italians from outside Rome (the 'New' Synagogue) at the top. The

Opposite, above: The Square of the Five Synagogues, Rome.
(*Jewish National and University Library, Jerusalem*)

Below: 'Temple' Synagogue, Rome, according to tradition established after the destruction of the Temple. Its interior, divided into three bays by twisted columns, was entirely of wood and the ark was of gilded wood. The synagogue burned down in 1893.
(*Courtesy of Centro di Cultura Ebraica, Rome*)

Opposite, below left: The reader's desk in the Italian synagogue, Venice, with Corinthian columns and access via a double staircase.
(*Judaica Photo Archive, Israel Museum, Jerusalem*)

Opposite, below right: The Catalan-Aragonese Synagogue, another of the five Roman synagogues, served Jews of Catalan and Aragonese origin. The ark, crowned by a seven-branched candelabrum and the tablets of the Law, was of wood with marble seats on either side. The synagogue was built in the sixteenth century and renovated in 1622–8.
(*Judaica Photo Archive, Israel Museum, Jerusalem*)

Above: The mid-sixteenth-century Italian Synagogue in Padua. The ark and raised reading desk are along the long walls and are thus close to one another.
(*Italian Jewish Museum – U. Nahon, Jerusalem*)

Left: The synagogue at Casale Monferrato, one of a group of synagogues in the Piedmont area, with the reader's desk in front of the ark.
(*Italian Jewish Museum – U. Nahon, Jerusalem*)

Above: The synagogue of Conegliano Veneto, 1701–19, whose furnishings were transferred to the Italian Synagogue, Jerusalem, in 1952.
(*Italian Jewish Museum – U. Nahon, Jerusalem*)

Right: The ark from the synagogue of Sermide, formerly in Mantua, carved in 1543. The ark is now in Jerusalem.
(*Italian Jewish Museum – U. Nahon, Jerusalem*)

Engraving of the interior of the Leghorn Synagogue, after extensive remodelling in 1789, with three tiers of arches, the rococo lattices of the women's galleries, imposing painted ceiling with gold-lettered inscriptions, lavishly decorated interior and gilded ark. The synagogue was destroyed by bombing during the Second World War.
(*Courtesy of Adolfo Toaff, Leghorn*)

building was also the home of the Jewish school and a library. There were occasional disagreements and tensions between the various congregations (as over problems of access: there was only one entrance allowed for the entire building and the 'Temple' Synagogue insisted on its exclusive right to use the main staircase in its wing). Nevertheless, the building remained Rome's sole synagogue for almost 350 years. It was only demolished following a disastrous fire in 1893 and new city planning of the area at the turn of the century. The building overlooked a square known as the Square of the Synagogues (Piazza delle Scole). Prints and documents have preserved information on these synagogues, and despite their humble environment it appears that outstanding Roman artists helped with the adornment and decorations. Many ritual objects have been preserved, some in Rome's modern Central Synagogue. They are artistic treasures often with inscriptions containing valuable information about their wealthy donors.

A different architectural type of synagogue was to be found in the Piedmont area. Here, under Ashkenazi influence, the reader's desk was in the centre of the hall and not against the western wall. The fine synagogue at Casale Monferrato was the prototype of this group. It was built in 1595 but basically restored early in the eighteenth century, as were most of the synagogues in this area.

Throughout Italy the story was similar. The Jews were confined in humiliating ghettos, yet their spirit proved indomitable. It was exemplified in their uninterrupted religious and cultural creativity and found material expression in the loving care which made their houses of worship into miniature works of art. Since the Second World War Italian Jewry has fallen on difficult times and many of the smaller communities have disappeared. Some of their magnificent ritual objects have been transferred to Israel where they are displayed in museums or incorporated into Israeli synagogues.

— 6 —

EASTERN EUROPE

BETWEEN the fourteenth and the sixteenth centuries the focus of Ashkenazi Jewish life moved eastward from Germany to Poland, where major synagogues were built from the late fourteenth century onwards. Cracow was the outstanding Polish centre, capital of the Jagiellon kings at the time, and it was there that the first monumental synagogues appeared.

The first, and largest, was the Old (Stara) Synagogue in the Kazimierz suburb of Cracow. According to tradition, it was originally built in the fifteenth century by Jews who had fled from anti-Jewish riots in Prague. They reproduced the twin-nave plan dominant in the synagogues of Western and Central Europe, notably in the Worms Synagogue and in the Altneuschul in

The Old (Stara) Synagogue, the oldest existing synagogue in Poland, in Kazimierz, a suburb of Cracow. It was damaged and plundered by the Germans during the Second World War and its courtyard was used for

executions. The building was repaired after the war and now serves as a Jewish Museum. (*Beth Hatefutsoth Archive, Tel Aviv/Photo: Tadeusz Kowalski*)

Above: The interior of the Old Synagogue in Cracow, showing its Gothic style and the cage-like wrought-iron enclosure of the reader's platform in the centre of the hall. Etching by Jan Wojnarski, early twentieth century. (*Beth Hatefutsoth Archive, Tel Aviv*)

Below: Praying at the tomb of Rabbi Moses Isserles, the Rema, on Lag ba-Omer in the cemetery adjoining the synagogue built in his honour. (*Menakhem Kipnis-Raphael Abramovich Collection, YIVO, New York*)

Prague. Cracow's Old Synagogue was Poland's 'mother' congregation. In its Gothic-style interior the great rabbinical and communal leaders and the heads of the rabbinical academies gathered and prayed. Here royal decrees affecting the community were read out, as were sentences of excommunication issued by the Jewish leaders on recalcitrant members.

Cracow, more than any other town in Eastern Europe, fell under the influence of the Italian Renaissance, and the Italian architects, builders and craftsmen who worked there combined Renaissance with local styles. The Florentine architect Matteo Gucci introduced changes in the spirit of the Cracow Renaissance into the Old Synagogue, probably after a disastrous fire in 1557. These are especially noticeable in exterior features such as the buttresses and parapet, which anticipate the later baroque fortress synagogues.

Other outstanding stone synagogues built in the sixteenth century were entirely in the Renaissance style. Cracow's Rema synagogue, first constructed in 1553 (and rebuilt after a fire a few years later), resembles numerous other Cracow buildings of the time such as monasteries, small churches and chapels. It was built by the father of the great rabbinical authority, Moses Isserles (the Rema), in honour of his son, and was one of a group of family synagogues in Poland financed by men of wealth and intended for a limited group of worshippers from the founding family.

The Hoyche ('High') Synagogue in Cracow, built late in the sixteenth century, is another classic example of Jewish Polish Renaissance religious art. The metal doors of its ark were sculpted by two Jewish artists, and paintings on biblical themes decorate – for the first time in more than a thousand years – a synagogue wall. The last of the great Renaissance synagogues in Cracow is the Isaac Jacobowicz (or Jekeles) Synagogue, opened in 1644. This barrel-vaulted hall was named after a rich banker who financed its construction. He originally obtained permission from the king in 1638 to build the synagogue but the work was

Rema Synagogue, Cracow, was one of the first Polish
synagogues in the Renaissance style. It was burned by
the Nazis but reconstructed after the war.
(*Beth Hatefutsoth model/Photo: Michael Horton*)

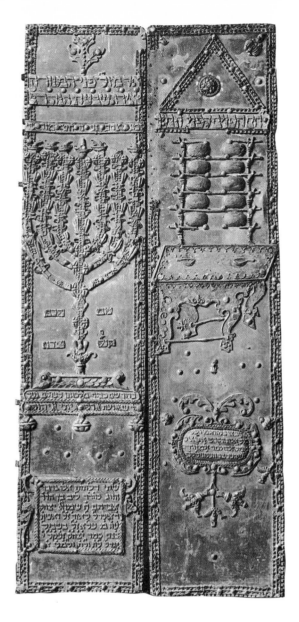

Left: The doors of the ark from the Hoyche ('High') Synagogue in Cracow, made of painted lead on wood, with depictions of ritual objects from the Temple. (*Israel Museum, Jerusalem*)

Above: Isaac Jacobowicz Synagogue in Cracow in the Renaissance style, probably designed by an Italian architect. The exterior porch covered the stairs leading to the women's gallery. (*Beth Hatefutsoth Archive, Tel Aviv*)

Right: Jews at prayer on the Day of Atonement: painting by Maurycy Gottlieb (1856–79) of a Yom Kippur service in a Cracow synagogue. (*Tel Aviv Museum*)

delayed for several years as the priests from a nearby church objected to passing a synagogue while carrying the sacraments.

Outside Cracow other monumental synagogues in Renaissance style appeared. The Isaac Nachmanowicz (or Taz) Synagogue, for example, was built in Lwow in 1582 by the Italian architect, Paolo Romano (who was also responsible for the city's combined Renaissance-Gothic Greek Orthodox Wallachian Church). Like the Rema Synagogue, the Taz was originally a family synagogue but it

was one of the largest and most splendid in the city. Its square shape was widely copied and was to become the norm in Polish synagogues. As in Italy, the Renaissance synagogues were usually rectangular and barrel-vaulted. The ark and reader's platform were free-standing furnishings which did not yet dominate the interior.

It was the growing concentration on the reader's platform that dictated a major development in Polish synagogue architecture. This platform, used as a pulpit for the preacher and

also for speakers at non-religious assemblies, achieved a significance transcending even that of the ark. Its central position was laid down by Moses Isserles as essential, and became an integral part of the design, thanks to the introduction of the four-pillared synagogue. The ceiling or dome of the building rested on four massive columns placed around the centre of the structure and the raised platform was constructed as an integral element joining the four columns. Although the four-pillar structure solution was inspired by the Italian Renaissance, its development and application were an original Jewish contribution. Indeed, for the first time since the classical period, over a thousand years earlier, Jews now emerged as synagogue builders and decorators. Basing themselves on Jewish religious tradition, they sought to move away from non-Jewish influences and to seek authentic Jewish expressions for their art. Although the introduction of the four pillars may appear an architectural technicality, its permanent fixing of the platform in the centre of the hall was an important contri-

bution to synagogue design. The focus now moved from the ornate design of the building to concentration on the ritual features, on the platform and the ark.

An outstanding example of the four-pillared synagogue was the Great Synagogue in Vilna. Vilna had been the site of one of the most distinguished early East European synagogues, the Old Klaus, constructed in the mid-fifteenth century. Its Great Synagogue, originally built of wood in 1573, was burned down in anti-Jewish riots in 1592. It was rebuilt in brick and stone, and various changes were introduced in the following years.

Most of the best-known Polish synagogues were constructed between the sixteenth and mid-seventeenth centuries. The climate of comparative religious freedom contributed to the spate of building. In the royal cities permission had to be received from the king and it was usually granted, although often hedged with restrictions imposed under pressure from the Church, which demanded that the king adhere to ancient legislation forbidding the erection of

Above: General view of the Vilna Shulhof (synagogue courtyard). The tall building at the back is the main synagogue adjoining the Strashun Library. The entire complex was partly destroyed in the Second World War and subsequently razed.
(Beth Hatefutsoth model/Photo: Michael Horton)

Opposite: Interior of the Great Synagogue, Vilna, a striking example of the 'four pillar' synagogue, in which the reading desk is built into the four columns supporting the ceiling. The platform between the pillars was in the form of a pavilion reached by a long staircase. The ark was also elevated, with access via a double staircase.
(Beth Hatefutsoth model/Photo: Michael Horton)

View from the Vilna Shulhof into Jews' Street, c.1930. The gate was at the entrance to the Shulhof which included over twenty synagogues and was the focus of community life. On the right is the entrance to the synagogue of the famous scholar, the Vilna Gaon, built in 1800 on the site of his home. On the left is the Strashun Library.
(*Central Archives for the History of the Jewish People, Jerusalem*)

new synagogues. The church protested vehemently at the appearance of 'vast new brick synagogues, more beautiful than previously and indeed comparable to churches'. The situation was easier in the private cities, owned by wealthy nobles, where the Church exerted less influence. Some restrictions were enforced – the synagogue had to be a considerable distance from the church, away from the town square, and often near the walls. But, apart from this, no other restrictions were imposed and these synagogues were often tall, prominent landmarks. The Jews were immensely proud of their places of worship which were the centre of their social as well as their religious life.

After the Renaissance and four-pillar styles, the baroque synagogue, often built as a fortress, emerged. The synagogues in Poland, especially those near the Russian and Ukrainian frontiers, were not only places for worship, study, and assembly but also, very often, for defence. Within the city they served not only as a refuge for Jews under attack, but were part of the city's general defensive net-work. On occasion, Jews were not allowed to build their synagogues within the town but had to construct them outside the walls. Thus freed of restrictions on height and size, these syn-agogues were often large and impressive build-ings, but they, too, had to incorporate a defence system against the all too frequent attacks.

The 'fortress' synagogues were monumental buildings with thick walls and escarpments. Most striking was the parapet, used not only as a lookout in time of trouble but for active defence: it was provided with loopholes for cannons and guns. The parapets were given an ornamental form with crenellated cornices and small towers and not all were intended for military use. Some of the indentations in the parapets were nothing more than rainspouts. In the Lutsk community in 1626, however,

Above: Interior of Lutsk Synagogue with the platform, covered by a stone canopy, integral to the four octagonal pillars that support the barrel-vaulted ceiling. (*Jewish National and University Library, Jerusalem*)

Below: A nineteenth-century engraving of the Lutsk fortress synagogue. The corner tower was reached by an interior staircase. (*Beth Hatefutsoth Archive, Tel Aviv*)

Fortress synagogue in Lutsk. Many synagogues
throughout Poland were designed to be defended in case
of need. Although the Catholic clergy of Lutsk objected
to permitting the Jews to build such an imposing
structure, they were overruled.
(*Beth Hatefutsoth model/Photo: Michael Horton*)

Mid-seventeenth-century wooden synagogue in
Zabludow. The Zabludow Synagogue was remodelled at
various times and its final appearance, the result of the
1756 rebuilding, reflected the style of the wooden
synagogue in Wolpa. The two prayer rooms for women
and a third one for the vestibule were each covered with
a separate roof.
(Beth Hatefutsoth model/Photo: Michael Horton)

military objectives were paramount in the permission granted by the king for the synagogue: it was to be equipped with 'embrasures or loopholes on all four sides, to be armed at the expense of the Jews and provided with able men to repulse enemy attacks'. The synagogue at Rszesow was ordered by the authorities to provide itself 'with rifles, bullets and gunpowder'. The fortress synagogues often had a tower at one corner; in times of emergency this was used as a lookout but otherwise served as a jail for criminals (synagogues often made provision for cells in their vestibules or cellars to imprison petty criminals). Architecturally, the parapet motif frequently recurs within the building, sometimes as a blind arcade on the walls underneath a row of windows. In these synagogues the platform, between the four pillars, is massive and impressive. The ark is much larger than in earlier Polish synagogues and is richly decorated with motifs taken from flora and fauna and even with human figures.

Another original contribution of Polish

Below: Fortress synagogue at Zolkiew, as rebuilt in 1692 when a masonry structure replaced the older wooden building. The parapet was adorned with turrets and indentations.
(*Beth Hatefutsoth Archive, Tel Aviv*)

Above: Fortress synagogue in Belz. This serves as the architectural inspiration for a synagogue now being built in Jerusalem by the followers of the *rebbe* of Belz. (*Archive for the Study of Hasidism, Jerusalem*)

Below: The reader's desk, enclosed by four pillars with dedicatory inscriptions, in the synagogue at Tykocin, built in 1672. (*Yad Vashem Archives, Jerusalem*)

Above: Corner of the fortress synagogue in Brody, built in the seventeenth century. (*Beth Hatefutsoth Archive, Tel Aviv*)

Below: Stone canopy over the platform in the Great Synagogue in Lancut, seventeenth century. The Crown of the Torah is carried by symbolic deer. (*Beth Hatefutsoth Archive, Tel Aviv/Photo: Nathan Beyrak*)

Above: The early eighteenth-century wooden synagogue in Wolpa, which was greatly admired and imitated. A towering three-tiered roof covered the main hall which was surrounded by lower structures, including women's prayer rooms along the northern and southern walls. On either side of the vestibule (*centre, front*) are two-storey corner pavilions with outside galleries.
(*Judaica Photo Archive, Israel Museum, Jerusalem*)

Opposite, above: Wooden synagogue in Jurburg, built in 1790.
(*Yad Vashem Archives, Jerusalem*)

Opposite, below: Wooden synagogue of Wizuny, Lithuania. Its two-tiered roof covers the entire structure, including the women's gallery which is reached by an interior staircase.
(*Beth Hatefutsoth Archive, Tel Aviv*)

Jewry was the wooden synagogue. Timber, usually pinewood but also oak, was in abundant supply in the forest regions, and wood was easy to work with. It was a popular building material and was used for humble dwellings, royal palaces and places of worship of all denominations – Catholic and Protestant, Greek Orthodox and Jewish. Although wooden synagogues were not pictorially documented before the mid-seventeenth century, they probably existed much earlier. The new communities, especially in the rural areas, were unable to afford masonry. At first they assembled for prayers in private homes and then they built synagogues of wood, which were not costly or difficult to construct. The builders were often Jewish and they were influenced by the styles prevalent in their environs as, for example, timber churches. The outstanding period of wooden synagogue building was from the mid-seventeenth to the late eighteenth centuries. Their vulnerability to fire and wood-rot, combined with the frequent havoc wrought by wars and anti-Jewish attacks, led to large-scale destruction. The ruined synagogues were often replaced by stone structures in the more solid communities which preferred building materials affording more security. About a hundred wooden synagogues survived until the Second World War but all were then razed by the Germans.

Architecturally, the design of the interior of

Wooden reader's platform in the synagogue at Zelwa.
(*Judaica Photo Archive, Israel Museum, Jerusalem*)

Below: Wooden platform for the reader in the synagogue
at Zabludow (mid-seventeenth century).
(*Photo: Szymon Zajczyk*)

these synagogues resembled that of stone synagogues. The use of space was similar, and emphasis placed on the main hall where the men prayed. A maximum monumental effect was achieved, for example, through the use of vaulted ceilings and, from the eighteenth century, sometimes by cupolas. Some timber synagogues even had four pillars around the platform, although they had no architectural function. The main hall towered above the other units and this feature distinguished the timber synagogue from the timber church. The women were consigned to subordinate quarters, usually a lean-to annexe where they heard the prayers through a small grilled window. Religious regulations demanded separate entrances for the women. When a women's gallery was incorporated, usually over the vestibule, it was reached by a special staircase, internal or external.

The wooden synagogues were built along two basic patterns. Most of those in central and southern Poland were rectangular with a single roof covering its three constituents, the main hall, the women's chamber, and the vestibule. Elsewhere, especially in the neighbourhoods of Bialystok and Grodno, the vestibule and women's room were separate annexes, surrounding the main hall on the southern, western, and northern sides. Although designed in accordance with local prototypes, the ornamentation reflected the originality and imagination of the Jewish craftsmen who, working in a spirit of holiness and reverence, poured of themselves into the graceful workmanship. Outside, the roof took on added importance as the number of tiers was extended; inside, every detail was lovingly crafted. This unique expression of Jewish folk art reached its zenith in the elaborate carvings and paintings that adorned the ark, the walls, and the ceiling. The themes were many and varied: plants, animals, and even human figures, Bible scenes, subjects such as the Temple vessels, Jewish legend, imaginary views of the Holy Land (especially Jerusalem), heraldic ornamentations and signs of the zodiac, and brief quotations from the

Scriptures and the sayings of the Rabbis, often enclosed in medallions, and artistically employing the Hebrew letter.

The wooden synagogues occupy a special place in the history of synagogue art in respect of their construction, design, and decoration. The buildings were not large and the work was modest, but the results were the unique and independent expression of Jewish craftsmen, some of whose names have been preserved. One of these, Hayyim ben Isaac Segal, inscribed on the dome of the Mohilev Synagogue dome the words:

It is for this reason that I have walked in the land of the living for many years. To fulfil my destiny by painting this dome. To honour our rabbi and our God, may He always save us from our enemies.

The nature of the material – wood – contributed to the rustic warmth which resulted and which conveyed the intimacy and charm of simple faith and the labour of love for the glorification of God. As one authority put it: 'The wooden synagogues reached the acme of the carpenters' art.'

The distinctive building styles of Polish synagogues were taken to other countries by the

Above: Wall-painting in the wooden synagogue of Grojec, illustrating verses from Psalm 137: 'By the rivers of Babylon, there we sat down, yea, we wept when we remembered Zion. Upon the willows ... we hung up our harps.' (The word translated as 'harps' was used for 'violins' in later Hebrew.)
(*Judaica Photo Archive, Israel Museum, Jerusalem*)

Below: Chodorow Synagogue in about 1900. Extensive restoration in 1909–10 altered its external appearance.
(*Tel Aviv Museum/Photo: Matias Berson*)

Jews of Poland, especially those fleeing the great pogroms of the mid-seventeenth century. They were now to be found, for example, in parts of Germany, Hungary and Bohemia, and are even reflected in the four-pillared Ashkenazi 'Ha-Ari' Synagogue in Safed, in northern Israel.

The rise of the pietist movement of Hasidism in the eighteenth century represented a protest against the all-powerful community organization and led to a changed attitude to the synagogue. The new sect was persecuted by the religious establishment and excluded from the existing houses of worship. In any case, the Hasidim adopted a different prayer rite which was regarded as heretical in the regular synagogues.

The followers of Hasidism gathered in a *shtiebl* (small room) which served for prayer, study, and assembly. Little or no attention was paid to the aesthetic aspects as the Hasidim sought to be oblivious of externals. The premises were austere in appearance and furnishings. The sound of the prayer and the movement of the body, expressing inner fervour and joy, were all that mattered. This was achieved through communal song and dance. (The followers of one Hasidic rabbi even jumped and turned somersaults while at prayer, but this was condemned by other groups.) From the outside the *shtiebl* resembled any other house in the vicinity, while externally it was nondescript. The *rebbe* gave his expositions from his seat next to a plain table. He needed no pulpit and his followers needed none of the trappings valued by other Jews. Even wealthy Hasidic Jews made no attempt to beautify their places of worship. The *shtiebls* had no distinctive form and made no contribution to Jewish synagogue architecture, but they soon proliferated, despite the bitter hostility of their opponents.

After the partition of Poland in the latter part of the eighteenth century Polish synagogue architecture lost its originality. The new buildings were usually small, oblong structures. The more impressive examples copied styles developed in Central Europe. Nevertheless, the synagogue never lost its central role as the focus of Jewish life in the *shtetl* (small town) and in the city, as a house of prayer and a house of assembly.

The *beth midrash* (study and prayer room) of Israel Baal Shem Tov, founder of Hasidim, in Medzibezh, Podolia. This modest building was typical of the simple, unadorned synagogues of the Hasidim.
(*Jewish National and University Library, Jerusalem*)

Interior of the wooden synagogue at Kirchheim, Germany (1739–40), one of a group of German wooden synagogues decorated by Jews from eastern Europe. This one was painted by Eliezer ben Solomon Sussman. (*Yad Vashem Archives, Jerusalem*)

Detail from the painted barrel-vaulted ceiling of the synagogue in Chodorow, Poland (today U.S.S.R.), showing medallions with Hebrew inscriptions linking the subjects of the pictures with the promise of redemption. This synagogue was originally built in the mid-seventeenth century but, according to an inscription, the paintings were executed by Israel ben Mordecai Lisnitski in 1714.
(Beth Hatefutsoth model/Photo: Michael Horton)

7

TOWARDS EMANCIPATION

In the West the seventeenth and eighteenth centuries brought with them innovations in synagogue design, influenced by the new spirit of Enlightenment. One of these was to affect the seating of female congregants (see Chapter X). Up to that time no provision had been made for them in many synagogues, as it was assumed that they would not attend. At best they were placed behind a curtain, partition, or wall. One example of the degraded position of women was in the synagogues of Provence, in southern France, where they were confined to a basement below the main hall. Light entered only through a grille leading to the upper room, and for the women the climax of the service came when the reader held the Scroll of the Law close to the grille for them to glimpse. In some places the women had their own reader who would recite the prayers for them in Provençal. Apart from the women's room, the lower level of the synagogues also contained the ritual bath and the bakery for *matzoth* (unleavened bread).

The Provençal synagogues dated from the Middle Ages but those at Carpentras and Cavaillon were rebuilt in the eighteenth century in the form in which they are known today. This included more appropriate arrangements for women, who were provided with their own gallery with access via a special stairway. Architecturally these synagogues are reminiscent of the one in Cordova, Spain, consisting of a broad hall, with the ark and platform at opposite ends. In Provence, however, the platform is raised to the height of a gallery and approached by two symmetrical staircases (as in some of the Italian synagogues). Both of the rebuilt synagogues are graceful halls, although their exteriors were deliberately kept modest in order to cloak their identity.

A synagogue in Carpentras was first erected in the thirteenth century after the Jews had received the necessary permission from the local bishop: in return, they had promised to provide him with sheets for his guest beds and the tongues of all slaughtered cattle. The synagogue was later turned into a church. A new one was built in 1367 after the Jews undertook to pay the bishop an annual tribute of six pounds of pepper. Later complaints were made that it was higher than the cathedral, so the roof had to be lowered. The eighteenth-century reconstruction included a roof terrace for outdoor ceremonies (such as blessing the moon and constructing the tabernacle). An unusual feature of the rococo-style interior is a small Louis XIV chair, known as the Chair of Elijah, placed in a niche a few feet up in the wall near the ark; it was too small to sit in but was ceremoniously taken to every circumcision. The smaller synagogue at Cavaillon, which

Façade of the second Cavaillon Synagogue, built in 1772 and incorporating parts of an earlier synagogue. (*Beth Hatefutsoth Archive, Tel Aviv/Photo: Studer, Cavaillon*)

resembles the Carpentras Synagogue, was first built in 1499 and bridges the entrance to the ancient Jewish ghetto.

The entry of the Jews into modern times was pioneered by Jews from Spain and Portugal, who had adopted a nominal Christianity until they could escape in the sixteenth and seventeenth centuries to more hospitable climes. As their new homes could not be Catholic lands where they would have been hunted down by the Inquisition, they went to the Protestant lands of western Europe and to the New World. In Europe they found welcome havens in Holland, England, and the Baltic ports of Germany. By the early seventeenth century those in the Netherlands were permitted to practise their religion freely, although at first they judiciously concealed their synagogues behind residential façades. By 1620, however, Amsterdam had three separate Sephardi congregations, all in the same neighbourhood, and all with buildings in the style of the city's Calvinist churches. With the opening of a fine new synagogue in 1639, the three congregations merged. The symbol chosen for the united congregation (still to be seen above the entrance to the present Portuguese Synagogue) was a pelican feeding her three young ones (representing the three congregations). The pelican was selected as a symbol of self-sacrifice since, according to legend, it feeds its hungry youngsters on its own blood. From artistic depictions we know that the 1639 building was an impressive structure, and contained galleries for the women.

It was in this synagogue that two of the most famous cases of excommunication in Jewish history occurred, Uriel da Costa (or Acosta) in 1624 and Baruch (Benedict) Spinoza in 1656. Excommunication was the most severe punishment that could be imposed by a Jewish court. The person convicted was forbidden entrance to the synagogue and all social contacts between him and other Jews were severed. The more dramatic of the two was the case of da Costa, who was twice excommunicated for

Opposite, far left: Interior of the Carpentras Synagogue, built in 1367 and extensively renovated in 1741–3. On the right is the reader's platform above the entrance, with three candelabra dating from the nineteenth century. Women sat in a grilled section below the open gallery in the southern wall.
(*Keter Publishing House, Jerusalem*)

Opposite: The Chair of Elijah in the Carpentras Synagogue, used for circumcision ceremonies.
(*Photo: R.H.Stern*)

Right: Façade of the Lunéville Synagogue, 1785. During the French Revolution the crown above the round window was removed.
(*Photo: Hernand, Lunéville*)

Below: Interior of the Cavaillon Synagogue. The reading desk is high in the western wall, supported by Corinthian columns and enclosed by a wrought-iron grille.
(*Beth Hatefutsoth Archive, Tel Aviv/Photo: Studer, Cavaillon*)

I. Veenhuysen Delineavit.

holding views regarded as heretical. When he subsequently recanted he was required to undergo a humiliating ritual in the synagogue, which he described as follows:

I entered the synagogue which was filled with curious spectators, men and women. I walked to the reading desk and read the form of confession which they had written for me in which I had to declare that I deserved a thousand deaths for the crimes I had committed and that I would submit to whatever sentence they decreed. The chief elder then directed me to a corner of the synagogue where I was stripped to the waist and put my arms around a pillar. The sexton then stepped forward and whipped me thirty-nine times with a leather-thonged whip, during which a psalm was recited. Then I was told to sit on the ground and an elder came and absolved me of my excommunication. Then I dressed, went to the entrance of the synagogue and lay down on the threshold. Now the entire congregation, young and old, passed over me, stepping on the lower part of my legs and making gestures that were more like monkeys than humans.

The humiliation proved too much for da Costa, who shortly afterwards committed suicide.

The edict of excommunication on the philosopher, Spinoza, was also read out in this synagogue. The communal leaders were strict in both these cases because they feared that their relations with the civic authorities would be damaged if they did not take strong steps against heretical views. Spinoza never recanted and lived the rest of his life banned from the community.

Opposite, above: Exterior of the Amsterdam Portuguese 'Talmud Torah' Synagogue, 1639. Corinthian pilasters extended to both floors of the dignified façade. Etching by Romeyn de Hooghe.
(Biblioteca Rosenthaliana, Amsterdam)

Opposite, below: Interior of the 'Talmud Torah' Synagogue, Amsterdam. The large nave was spanned by four timber barrel vaults. The galleries were supported by Doric columns and divided into sections with grilles for the women (closer to the ark) and open sections for men. The silver chandeliers were lit on High Holidays. Etching by I. Veehuysen, *c.*1660.
(Joods Historisch Museum, Amsterdam)

By 1670 the synagogue was already too small for the rapidly growing congregation and it was decided to build a larger one (the former one became a banquet hall). In 1671 four foundation stones were laid by four worthies of the congregation (who had made appropriate donations) for whom special prayers were thereafter recited every year on the anniversary of the ceremony. The practice of laying four cornerstones for a new synagogue was later followed by other Sephardi congregations, notably in the Caribbean and the United States of America.

The Portuguese Synagogue (the 'Esnoga') was dedicated in 1675 in a ceremony with choir and orchestra followed by six days of celebrations which included sermons by the rabbi and all his pupils. At that time it was the largest synagogue in the world and it remains an Amsterdam landmark (although today it is seldom used for services). The spacious hall (125 ft × 95 ft) seats over 1,200 men and more than four hundred women are accommodated in the women's galleries. Four large columns on either side support the barrel-vaulted ceiling while another six smaller columns sustain the galleries which run around three sides of the building. The baroque-style ark is an impressive composition made of jacaranda wood brought from Brazil. The same wood was used for the reader's platform close to the entrance in the western wall. (For a long time Ashkenazi visitors were confined to the area behind this platform.) The general architectural design reflects contemporary Dutch style which was influenced by Calvinism (so-called 'Protestant baroque'). Some of the details were inspired by a wooden model of the Temple of Solomon, made by the Amsterdam Jew, Jacob Judah Aryeh Leon, which was very popular about the time the synagogue was being designed. During the day the Esnoga's seventy-two windows ensured bright light, and in the evenings hundreds of candles, on magnificent chandeliers and in candlesticks on each bench, lit up the interior. (Even today no electricity has been installed to mar this effect.) Around the

Above: Exterior of the Portuguese Synagogue
(the 'Esnoga'), Amsterdam, 1671–5. The outstanding
synagogue of its time, its design was copied
Sephardi communities in western Europe and
America.
(Beth Hatefutsoth model/Photo: Michael Horton)

Opposite: Interior of the Portuguese Synagogue,
Amsterdam. Tall, stately columns support the roof;
smaller ones support the women's gallery. Along
the far wall are places of honour for the officers of
the community.
(Beth Hatefutsoth model/Photo: Michael Horton)

spacious courtyard is a group of ancillary buildings including a school, community offices, the rabbinate, and the famous Ets Haim Library which still retains its seventeenth-century old-world atmosphere.

Jews from Central Europe began to arrive in Amsterdam shortly after the Jews from Portugal, and their main synagogue was dedicated in 1671, four years before the Esnoga. It was located directly across the canal from where the new Esnoga was being built. (The canal has since been replaced by a motorway.) It is a fine brick building, strongly influenced by its surroundings (its architect had built the Amsterdam Town Hall). Later, three other Ashkenazi synagogues were established in the immediate vicinity. Although they ceased to function during the Second World War and remained neglected for several decades, they are now being restored, and the complex of the four Ashkenazi synagogues will house Amsterdam's Jewish Historical Museum.

Above: The Day of Atonement in the Ashkenazi Great Synagogue, Amsterdam. Engraving by Bernard Picart, 1725.
(*Joods Historisch Museum, Amsterdam*)

Opposite: Sounding the *shofar* in the Portuguese Synagogue, Amsterdam. In front of the reader's desk is the rabbi of the congregation. Engraving by Bernard Picart, 1725.
(*Joods Historisch Museum, Amsterdam*)

Left: Amsterdam Portuguese Synagogue, built in 1675 (*left*) facing the Ashkenazi Great Synagogue, the two separated by a canal. Detail of an engraving by A. van der Laan, *c.*1670.
(*Biblioteca Rosenthaliana, Amsterdam*)

The Amsterdam Portuguese Synagogue was the 'mother synagogue' of a group of houses of worship in the western Sephardi world, of which one of the best-known was built in London. Jews had been expelled from England in 1290 and only returned, with the consent of Oliver Cromwell, in 1656. At first they rented a house in Creechurch Lane with the rabbi's residence on the ground floor and the prayer hall upstairs. The women sat in an adjoining room and one Christian visitor, glimpsing them through the partition, described his impression of them, 'in rich silks daubed with broad gold lace, with muffs on one hand and books in the other'. The Creechurch Lane Synagogue became one of the sights of London and the stream of Christian visitors proved such a nuisance that an ordinance was issued as follows: 'to avoid the scandal and hindrance caused when English ladies come to see the ceremonies of our religion, it is forbidden and ordained that no member of the Holy Congregation may bring them to it, nor rise nor move from his place to receive them'.

One of the visitors was the diarist, Samuel Pepys, who was taken there on the Feast of the Rejoicing of the Law in 1663 and was shocked by what he saw:

After dinner my wife and I, by Mr. Rawlinson's conduct, to the Jewish Synagogue; where the men and boys in their veils, and the women behind a lattice out of sight; and some things stand up, which I believe is their Law, in a press, to which all coming in do bow; and in the putting on their veils do say something, to which the others that hear him do cry, Amen, and the party do kiss his veil. Their all in a singing way and in Hebrew. And anon their Laws that they take out of the press are carried by several men, four or five several burdens in all, and they do relieve one another; and whether it is that every one desires to have the carrying of it, thus they carried it round about the room while such a service is singing. And in the end they had a prayer for the King, which they pronounced his name in Portuguese; but the prayer, like the rest, was in Hebrew. But Lord! to see the disorder, laughing, sporting, and no attention, but confusion in all their service, more like brutes than people knowing the true God, would make a man forswear ever seeing them more; and indeed I never did see so much, or could have imagined there had been any religion in the whole world so absurdly performed as this.

By 1701 the Spanish and Portuguese Jews were an accepted and affluent element in London and had built their own synagogue in Bevis Marks in the East End, where they still worship today. The exterior is of red brick and the interior (80 ft × 50 ft) is patterned on the Amsterdam model. It has many similar features, such as the latticed women's gallery along three sides, the Tablets of the Law above the ark, the brass chandeliers, and the positioning of the reader's desk close to the western wall. Certain aspects, however, recall English Protestant meeting houses, while the President's chair is Chippendale. According to tradition, one of the beams in the roof was presented by the king, William III. On the day of the opening, the builder, a Quaker, returned all the profit he had made: he did not feel that it was justified to make money from constructing a house of worship to the universal God.

The Ashkenazim in London formed their own congregations and by the early eighteenth century had established several synagogues. Outstanding among them was the Great Synagogue in Duke's Place, dedicated in 1790 on the site where a more modest structure was previously in use. The reading desk was in the centre of the hall and behind it were benches for worshippers (whose view of the ark was blocked by the platform). The main seats were in front of the southern and northern walls. The building was destroyed by bombing during the Second World War.

Other synagogues directly inspired by the Amsterdam Esnoga were built in the Caribbean. In the early seventeenth century Sephardi Jews from Holland had followed the trade routes to Brazil and founded a community there. But when the Spanish reconquered the region, bringing the Inquisition in their wake, the Jews left. Most returned to Holland but some fled to the Caribbean where they established pioneer New World communities. The

Right: The Great Synagogue, Duke's Place, London, built by Ashkenazim and dedicated in 1790. A brick building, it seated 500 on the main floor and 250 in the galleries. Aquatint by A.C.Pugin and Thomas Rowlandson, *c.*1819.
(*Keter Publishing House, Jerusalem*)

Below: Bevis Marks Synagogue, established by the Sephardi community in London in 1700. As in Amsterdam, the ark is a two-storeyed chest surmounted by the Tablets of the Law. Watercolour by I.M.Belisario, *c.*1817.
(*Spanish and Portuguese Congregation, London*)

first such Jewish settlement was in Surinam. Here the Jews developed a region in the jungle called 'Joden-Savanne' ('The Jews' Savanna'), with plantations bearing such biblical names as Carmel, Hebron, and Sukkot. A Christian visitor in 1828 described the synagogue in the capital, Jerusalem-by-the-Riverside, as a strong brick building with pointed gables, a large ark with eighteen scrolls, and a women's gallery. In the course of time this whole area was deserted and became overgrown, but recently the shell of this synagogue was repaired and restored by a group of volunteers who were descendants of the original settlers.

Two large synagogues still stand in Surinam's capital, Paramaribo. The first built was Neveh Shalom, finished in 1723. A year later the congregation split over matters of religious observance and the Portuguese Jews built a second synagogue, Zedek ve-Shalom.

Neveh Shalom was rebuilt in the nineteenth century and is one of the outstanding buildings in Surinam. Zedek ve-Shalom was repaired on several occasions but never rebuilt and so today retains its historical authenticity.

The best-known Caribbean synagogue is Mikve Israel, consecrated in Curaçao in 1732. The congregation was founded in 1659 by a group of Jews from Amsterdam, headed by a nephew of Uriel da Costa who had taken a Torah scroll with him. The community's first rabbi, Josiau Pardo, had been a classmate of Spinoza. The Curaçao community served as the centre of the region in the following centuries, and at one time was the largest in the Western Hemisphere. The synagogue is a four-storey building standing in a tiled courtyard. A master carpenter was brought from Amsterdam to participate in the construction. The building shows the influence of both the

Above: Zedek va-Shalom Synagogue of the Dutch Ashkenazi Community in Paramaribo, Surinam. (*Beth Hatefutsoth Archive, Tel Aviv*)

Opposite: A view of the 'Joden Savanne', the Jewish settlement in the Surinam jungle. The building on the hill is probably the synagogue. Aquarelle by the French artist Benoit, who visited Surinam in 1839. (*Courtesy of Mordechai Arbell, Jerusalem*)

Right: Neveh Shalom Synagogue in Paramaribo, Surinam. The synagogue was made of wood, the cheapest and most available material. As in other Caribbean Sephardi Synagogues, the floor was covered with sand. (*Beth Hatefutsoth Archive, Tel Aviv/Photo: Micha Bar-Am*)

Mikve Israel Synagogue, Curaçao. The congregation was established in 1659 but this, its second synagogue, was dedicated only in 1732. It is still used by the small local community and by tourists.
(*Beth Hatefutsoth Archive, Tel Aviv/Photo: Micha Bar-Am*)

Interior of the Mikve Israel Synagogue, Curaçao. Its design is notably similar to the Portuguese Synagogue in Amsterdam.
(*Beth Hatefutsoth Archive, Tel Aviv/Photo: Micha Bar-Am*)

Portuguese Synagogue in Amsterdam and Spanish baroque. As the cost of the building exceeded the estimates, the members sent their slaves to help the labourers.

A curious tradition developed in the Sephardi synagogues of the Caribbean (in Curaçao, Surinam, Jamaica, and St Thomas), of covering the floors with sand (at one time brought especially from the Holy Land). Some say that the sand symbolizes the destruction of the Temple, some the wanderings in the desert, and some ascribe it to the time when the Marranos sought to deaden the sound of their prayer from the ears of the officers of the Inquisition. But it is most likely that it was used simply for reasons of cleanliness (the same usage can be found in churches of the region).

Synagogue life was taken very seriously in Curaçao. Some of its controversial aspects can be gathered from the rules issued by the community elders at different times:

On leaving the Synagogue, every person wishing to converse shall do so without raising his voice as otherwise it might be construed as quarrelling.

If a man gives sufficient cause to be ordered out of the Synagogue, no one shall arise from his seat to offend or defend him.

Fathers are forbidden to take their sons to their seats or to bring them in through the window or to take them to the women's synagogue. All boys are supervised by the appropriate officer with full power to punish boys who are boisterous in the Synagogue.

No one may enter the Synagogue with a club, sword, or dagger on pain of a penalty to be paid to the poor.

Punishments incurred for not attending the Synagogue: a fine followed by excommunication for refusal to pay it; denial of the wife's use of the ritual baths, of circumcision to his sons and of burial to him or any near relative.[1]

The Curaçao community was so wealthy that it helped to fund the establishment of the Jewish settlements that began to emerge in the late seventeenth and eighteenth centuries in North America. For a long time the Jews of New Amsterdam, like other non-Dutch residents, were denied their own house of worship and presumably prayed in private homes. A map of 1695 shows a synagogue in Beaver Street, New York, but the first building on record belonged to the Shearith Israel Congregation on Mill Street (now South William Street), opened in 1730. It was a masonry building 33 ft square, and some of its ritual objects can be seen in the congregation's present building on Central Park West.

The oldest synagogue in North America still in use is the Touro Synagogue in Newport, Rhode Island (named after its first cantor and his sons who endorsed it generously). The dean of American colonial architects, Peter Harrison, volunteered to design the synagogue (although he had previously never even been in one). The dedication ceremony in 1763 moved the local newspaper to write:

The Order and Decorum, the Harmony and Solemnity of the Musick, together with a handsome Assembly of People, in a Edifice the most perfect of the Temple kind perhaps in America, & splendidly illuminated, could not but raise in the Mind a faint Idea of the Majesty and Grandeur of the Ancient Jewish Worship mentioned in Scripture.

When George Washington visited Newport in

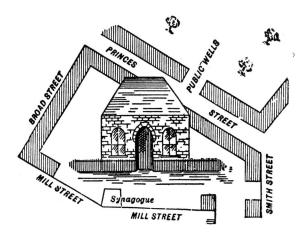

Sketch of the site of the Mill Street Synagogue, New York. Dedicated in 1730, for many years it was the only synagogue in the United States.
(*Jewish Encyclopedia, New York, 1905*)

1780, he was addressed by the Newport congregation and his reply was a classic statement of religious tolerance. In gratitude, his portrait was hung in a side room off the synagogue gallery where it remains to this day.

The synagogue itself (35 ft × 40 ft) is a masterpiece of Georgian colonial architecture. It stands inconspicuously on a side street with a plain brick exterior, now painted grey. Inside, twelve Ionic columns, representing the twelve tribes, support the women's gallery, and above these rise twelve Corinthian columns supporting the domed ceiling. Originally the sole seating for the men was the wainscoted bench running along the sides of the hall. In the floor of the reader's platform in the centre of the building is a trap-door which leads to the foundations, giving rise to the legend that runaway slaves escaped via the synagogue. In 1946 the Touro Synagogue was declared a National Historic Site.

Other early synagogues in North America included Mikveh Israel in Philadelphia (*c*.1745), Beth Elohim in Charleston, South Carolina (1794), Mikveh Israel in Savannah, Georgia (perhaps as early as 1733), and Shearith Israel in Montreal. (The Montreal congregation was founded in 1768; its first

1. Isaac S. and Suzanne E. Emmanuel, *The History of the Netherlands Antilles*, American Jewish Archives no. 5, Cincinnati 1970.

Above: Interior of Beth Elohim Synagogue, Charleston, South Carolina, *c.*1750, which was destroyed by fire in 1838. This lithograph, after a painting by S.N.Carvalho, shows the arrangement of the columns in two tiers, the elegant ark and the reader's oval desk.
(*Jewish Division, New York Public Library, Astor, Lennx and Tilden Foundations*)

synagogue was opened in 1777 on land donated by thirteen-year-old David David, the first Jew born in Canada, who had inherited it from his father, Lazarus David.) These early colonial synagogues, none of which survives, were built in the Sephardi pattern. Although by 1730 Ashkenazi Jews were in the majority, the communities were not large enough to support two congregations and so the Ashkenazim accommodated themselves to the synagogues of the earlier arrivals.

The Sephardi synagogues of Western Europe, the Caribbean, and North America were the harbingers of the new style of building that was to emerge with the Emancipation, the turning-point in Jewish history which saw the obtaining of civil rights, the emergence from the ghetto, and the entrance of the Jew into the society of his non-Jewish fellows.

Below: Shearith Israel, the Spanish and Portuguese Synagogue in Montreal. Shearith Israel was one of the first six congregations in North America and this building was dedicated in 1838.
(*Lawrence Lande Collection, Canada*)

Above: Exterior of the Touro Synagogue, Newport, Rhode Island, dedicated in 1763 and designed by Paul Harrison, designer of several civic buildings and churches in Newport. Harrison adopted an English Georgian style marked by symmetry, balance and ordered rhythm. The synagogue stands diagonally on its small plot so that the worshipper faces Jerusalem. (*Beth Hatefutsoth model/Photo: Michael Horton*)

Right: Interior of the Touro Synagogue, Newport. Five large brass candelabra hang from the ceiling; in front of the ark is the eternal light. Above the ark are the Ten Commandments in Hebrew, painted by the Newport artist Benjamin Howland. A portrait of George Washington hangs in a room off the gallery (*top left*). (*Beth Hatefutsoth model/Photo: Michael Horton*)

8

IN MOSLEM LANDS

FROM the seventh century, when the armies of Islam swept out of the Arabian peninsula and overran the Middle East and North Africa, reaching even into Europe, a large section of the Jewish people lived under Moslem rule. Jews, like Christians, were treated as second-class citizens, although, as 'People of the Book', both were accorded a more favoured status than pagans. Attitudes varied according to time and place: in Moslem Spain the Jews generally flourished but a period of fanaticism in the twelfth century led to the wholesale destruction of synagogues in North Africa and Spain. As early as the seventh century, Omar, the second caliph, forbade the building of any new synagogues or the repair of old ones in lands under Moslem rule. The ninth-century caliph, al-Mutawakkil, ordered that Jewish and Christian houses of worship built after the advent of Islam be destroyed (unless they were spacious structures, in which case they were to be turned into mosques). In the eleventh century Caliph al-Hakim decreed the demolition of all synagogues in Palestine. Although such harshness was not applied uniformly, the prevailing uncertainty discouraged the investment of resources in the construction of monumental synagogues. On the contrary, the Jews generally sought anonymity for their houses of worship in the hope that they would escape notice and be left in peace. Some fine buildings

were erected but the small, modest prayer-rooms which reflected both the political instability and the poverty of the Jewish masses were more usual.

Ways were found to circumvent the restriction on establishing new places of worship and the number of synagogues readily increased, especially in the larger communities, for example, Kairouan, Baghdad, Cairo, and Fez. Sometimes differences of opinion led to splits in existing congregations, but the main reason for proliferation was natural growth, as synagogues became too small even for their own constituents, not to mention Jews coming from elsewhere. The process can be illustrated by the number of synagogues in the main centres of sixteenth-century Turkey. In Istanbul, for example, there were three 'old-time' congregations, separate synagogues for Jews from each of the various parts of the Iberian peninsula (Castile, Catalonia, Aragon, Cordova, Granada and Portugal), synagogues for people from other parts of Turkey and Asia Minor, Greece, Italy (Calabria, Messina, Sicily, etc.), Bulgaria and Hungary, not to mention Ashkenazim and Karaites, as well as synagogues for various trade and guild groupings (such as the drapers' congregation). When the ban on synagogues was strongly enforced, prayer rooms would be established in private homes. If discovered by the authorities they would be

Tiferet Israel (or Nissim Beck) Synagogue, dedicated in 1865, rising above the Jewish Quarter of Jerusalem, 1937.
(*Keren Hayesod, Jerusalem*)

Bikkur Holim Synagogue, Izmir, Turkey.
(*Photo: Lorenzo Salzman*)

Hevra Synagogue, Izmir, Turkey.
(*Photo: Lorenzo Salzman*)

closed down and their contents confiscated. Sometimes the synagogues were the objects of savage attacks, but these were in violation of the code laid down by the caliph Omar and on occasion the authorities subsidized their repair.

Despite the wide geographical areas involved and the great number of local variants, some common characteristics can be discerned in the synagogues of Moslem countries. Since, for example, the Moslems insisted that the tops of the synagogues should be lower than the lowest mosque in the vicinity, the Jews of Moslem lands, as of Europe, often lowered the floor level to achieve internal height. In most synagogues the reader's platform stood in the centre of the hall, with the congregation seated around, facing the ark or the platform. Often a bench would line the walls but it was common for the men to sit on the floor, which was covered with carpets or mats. In some places the carpets were richly woven; in others, where the congregation was poor, the mats were plain and sometimes did not even cover the entire floor.

Multiple arks were common in oriental synagogues. Triple arks were usual but larger synagogues might have even more. Sometimes there was a niche on either side of the ark for prayerbooks. Interior decorations ranged from simple whitewashing to brightly-painted walls to elegant ornamentation, such as tiled arks, influenced by Moslem art styles. A profusion of plaques and inscriptions recorded verses from the Psalms or tributes to donors, while many designs had Cabbalistic origins, including renderings of the name of God or Psalm 67 written in the shape of a seven-branched candelabrum.

All synagogues had perpetual lamps, which burnt olive or sesame oil. In poorer areas, such as the Atlas Mountains, candles were placed in bowls. (In modern times the perpetual lamp is electric, although in some places its 'perpetuity' is comparative as it is only switched on at prayer time.) There was often an abundance of collection boxes, each representing a different communal philanthropic activity. At certain times during the prayers, or at their conclusion, the worshippers would insert coins.

Most synagogues had many Scrolls of the Law and whenever a distinguished member of

Bringing the Torah Scrolls to the dedication ceremony of
the Great Talmud Torah Synagogue in Salonica, 1900.
(*Yad Ben-Zvi, Jerusalem*)

the community died a new scroll would be written in his memory. The Great Synagogue in Baghdad, for example, had more than seventy scrolls, some of them kept in precious gold or silver boxes. On the Festival of the Rejoicing of the Law all were taken out and the entire congregation, men, women, and children, filed past, kissing each scroll. Every scroll was kept in its own container of carved wood or engraved metal, and even when being read from the reader's desk, it remained in its box, standing in an upright position. When a man was called to the Reading of the Law, it was customary for his sons to stand up, out of respect for him, until he returned to his seat. They would also rise for a grandfather or elder brother or other senior relative. To finance the synagogue, certain privileges, including the honour of being called to the Reading of the Law, were sold.

Wherever possible, synagogues had court-yards so that access would not be directly from the street. In the absence of a courtyard there was a vestibule. The courtyard often contained a water source, either a well or a tap, for purposes of ritual cleanliness, such as the washing of hands by the priests before they gave their blessing. In most places the Jews, under the influence of their Moslem environment, removed their shoes before entering the prayer hall. Shoes were either piled up by the entrance or kept in special racks or lockers in the courtyard or vestibule.

Prayers generally commenced very early. In Yemen, for example, the worshippers would arrive on the Sabbath three hours before dawn in order to read special prayers and cabbalistic literature until the regular service began, after daybreak. It was also customary to remain after prayers for a period of study. In some places a regular reader officiated. More frequently, any member of the community could lead the prayers provided he had a pleasant voice and was familiar with the melodies. The congregation knew most of the prayers by heart and much of the service was chanted in unison.

These synagogues usually had a women's section, although there were exceptions; in Yemen, for example, the women – who were not taught to pray – stood outside the door to watch the Scroll of the Law being taken out of the ark. Elsewhere, the women would sit at the back of the hall, often but not always behind a

General view of the el-Ghariba Synagogue in Djerba.
(*Beth Hatefutsoth Archive, Tel Aviv/Photo: Jan Parik*)

partition. In the summer it was commonplace for the women to sit outside and listen to the service through the windows.

A consideration of the main regions shows varying patterns in synagogue design. The North African coastal cities, for example, were open to European influences, and Spanish influences can be traced in the high platforms of the old synagogues in Algiers. On the whole, however, Spanish influence in synagogue construction was overshadowed by Islamic influence. One of the most famous synagogues in North Africa was the al-Ghariba ('The Wonderful'), on the island of Djerba, off the coast of Tunisia, whose Jewish community had lived there since ancient times. The Jews were concentrated in two all-Jewish villages, one having sixteen small synagogues, the other eight. All the scrolls on the island, however, were kept in the arks of al-Ghariba, which was a mile outside one of the villages. For Torah readings the Jews had to go to the main synagogue.

The Moorish-style, brightly-decorated al-Ghariba is probably the most sanctified synagogue in North Africa, also revered by the Moslems. It is the object of a mass pilgrimage on the holiday of Lag ba-Omer when visitors come from all over North Africa. In recent years this has attracted many former North African Jews now living in France and Israel, and is the one occasion when women attend, but since there is no women's section they sit in an outer room to listen to explanations of the festival. The crowds on Lag ba-Omer are so tightly packed that a police station is kept open for the day in the outer hall, in case of emergency.

According to tradition, the Jews of Djerba are divided into two congregations. Those from the south are reputed to have been descended from the ancient seafaring tribe of Zebulun who arrived by boat at the time of King Solomon. Those from the north – all supposedly of priestly descent – came after the destruction of the Temple, bringing with them

Above: The Great Synagogue in the Jewish Quarter of Tunis, thought to have been built six centuries ago and considered the oldest in the city. It has been restored many times.
(*Courtesy of Angel Lumbroso, Paris*)

Below: The interior of the Great Synagogue, Tunis.
(*Courtesy of Angel Lumbroso, Paris*)

Opposite: Danan Synagogue, Fez, built in the mid-seventeenth century and renovated in its present form at the end of the nineteenth century. To the left are the double arks; to the right is the reader's desk in the western wall.
(*Beth Hatefutsoth model/Photo: Michael Horton*)

Above: One of the reader's desks in the Aleppo Great Synagogue.
(*Beth Hatefutsoth model/Photo: Michael Horton*)

Right: The main synagogue in Aleppo, probably dating from the ninth century. In the central internal courtyard was a roofed pavilion which served as the reader's desk. There were seven arks: three in the west wing, three in the courtyard and the 'Sephardi ark' in the east wing.
(*Beth Hatefutsoth model/Photo: Michael Horton*)

one of its purported gates. This now stands in the al-Ghariba Synagogue. The building itself has been repaired on many occasions and it is difficult to distinguish its earlier forms. The al-Ghariba has also inspired many legends. In its pillared outer hall, for example, one of the pillars is missing and the arch hangs in mid-air. One legend insists that this was a deliberate omission to commemorate the destruction of the Temple. Another claims that there is a curse on anyone trying to correct the imperfection and that several people were struck dead in the attempt. The last one to suffer this fate was a workman from Italy, and his tools are still shown to visitors.

All the other synagogues on the island consist of a prayer hall and a colonnaded courtyard around an open space. The al-Ghariba, however, has two halls; when its congregation outgrew the original synagogue, the courtyard was presumably converted into a second hall. It has three entrances which lead from the outer hall to the prayer hall, one of a number of features which it has in common with the ancient Galilean synagogues; and some authorities suggest that its design was influenced by the Palestinian synagogues.

There are major synagogues in other parts of North Africa, such as in Tunis, where the Great Synagogue is reputedly six centuries old (although it is impossible to ascertain whether any part of the original structure still remains). In Libya there are also some synagogues in caves (in certain areas Jews even lived in caves). In a number of rural areas the synagogues owned olive plantations from which they pressed the oil for their lamps, the surplus being sold.

The synagogues of Cairo were particularly famous. On his visit to Fostat (Old Cairo), the twelfth-century traveller Benjamin of Tudela found two synagogues: one for 'the men of Israel', the other for the 'men of Babylonia' (i.e., of Iraqi origin). The main difference between the two was that the former completed the reading of the Pentateuch once a year, whereas the latter observed a triennial

cycle to go through the Torah readings. This difference notwithstanding, they joined to pray together twice a year, on the festival of Shavuot (marking the giving of the Torah) and on Simhat Torah (the Feast of the Rejoicing of the Law). The synagogue of 'the men of Israel' was built in 882 on the remains of the basilica of a Coptic church that had been sold to the Jews. It became known as the Synagogue of Elijah the Prophet and as the Ben Ezra Synagogue. Large-scale festivities were held there after the festivals of Passover and Tabernacles when it was the goal of pilgrimages made from various parts of North Africa. Its magnificently carved wooden doors have been brought to Israel and are to be seen at the Israel Museum in Jerusalem. The most famous Jew of the Middle

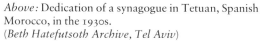

Above: Dedication of a synagogue in Tetuan, Spanish Morocco, in the 1930s.
(*Beth Hatefutsoth Archive, Tel Aviv*)

Right, above: The interior of Ben Ezra Synagogue, Cairo.
(*Beth Hatefutsoth Archive, Tel Aviv/Photo: Micha Bar-Am*)

Right: The doors of the Ben Ezra Synagogue, Cairo, with sixteen wood-carved panels probably dating from the eleventh century, now housed in Jerusalem.
(*Israel Museum, Jerusalem*)

Above: Prophet Elijah Synagogue, Alexandria, which was in existence by the fifteenth century.
(*Israel Museum, Jerusalem*)

Below: At prayer in the Karaite Synagogue, Cairo. The unfurnished hall and the prostrated worshippers betray Islamic influence.
(*Beth Hatefutsoth Archive, Tel Aviv/Photo: Micha Bar-Am*)

Ages, Moses Maimonides, philosopher, authority on religious law, medical writer, and communal leader, worshipped at this synagogue, as a result of which it was popularly called the Maimonides Synagogue. Next door, a small rabbinical academy was turned into a miraculous healing place for the sick.

In the 1890s, because the Maimonides Synagogue was in a state of extreme dilapidation, an extensive restoration programme was undertaken which resulted in one of the most exciting discoveries of Jewish scholarship. In an upper room, sealed off for centuries, a medieval *geniza* ('hiding-place') was found.

נוֹפֵ יֵשׁ בְּכָה בֵית בַכְנֶסֶת גְדוֹלָה וִיפָה אֵין עֶרוֹך אֵלֶיהָ וְיֵשׁ בָה חֲצֵר גְדוֹלָה וְבָה ב׳ תֵיבוֹת א׳רם

נָאִית וְשׁ אֵילָן שֶל תָמָר וּכְרִיתִיס וְתַחַתָּלֵי יִתְ קְרֵיהֵס וְעֵבֶר לְאַחֵר יֵשׁ פַרְדֵס וִתַחַתָּלֵי סֵם קַיְץ ׃

Above: Reader's desk in the Aleppo Great Synagogue as depicted by the sixteenth-century Jewish traveller known as the 'Casale Pilgrim', who wrote in his diary: 'In Aleppo there is a large and beautiful synagogue to which none other can be compared. Inside is a great courtyard with two fair lecterns and a date-tree and vines under which they pray. On the other side is an orchard, where they pray in the summer.' (C.Roth, 'The Casale Pilgrim', London, 1929)
(*Cecil Roth Collection*)

Below: A reader's desk in the courtyard of the Aleppo Great Synagogue.
(*Archive of Jewish Ethnography, Israel Museum, Jerusalem*)

Most synagogues had a *geniza* where damaged or worn-out scrolls of the Law and sacred books were put away or buried, but the Cairo Geniza proved unique. It contained a treasure trove of tens of thousands of documents including unknown masterpieces of ancient Hebrew literature as well as everyday records which threw vivid light on all aspects of Middle Eastern Jewish life in the Middle Ages.

Another ancient synagogue still standing in Cairo belongs to the Karaite Jews. This sect, which emerged in the eighth century, rejected the Oral Law and rabbinical interpretations, and relied only on the literal meaning of the

Entrance to the Great Synagogue in Baghdad. In the
doorway is the distinguished sage, Rabbi Ezra Reuven
Dangoor.
(*Yad Ben-Zvi, Jerusalem*)

Bible text. Although their customs, liturgy, and
calendar differed from those of the 'Rabbanites', their synagogues were similar.

Under Mameluke rule (thirteenth to sixteenth centuries) synagogues in the Middle East
were small and poor, indistinguishable from
their surroundings and often no more than
ruins. Although they were frequently much too
small for the community, they had to meet all
communal needs as the authorities forbade
their extension or the erection of new buildings. The traveller Obadiah of Bertinoro found
two old synagogues in Alexandria in 1487, one
large and one small. But the community of
twenty-five families preferred the smaller one
because the prophet Elijah, after whom it was
named, was reputed to have visited it. A
Turkish rabbi wrote in the sixteenth century:
'We are not allowed to have a permanent home
for a synagogue and certainly not to build one,
and we must hide in a low place and our voices

may not be outside, especially if someone is
living overhead.' Gallant attempts were made
to relieve the drab poverty by hanging up
brightly coloured lights within.

Conditions in Syria were similar. There, the
best-known old synagogues were to be found in
Damascus and Aleppo. The main synagogue in
Aleppo, allegedly built in the fifth century but
more likely dating from the ninth, resembled
the famous Cairo mosques in its layout. In the
central internal courtyard stood a raised,
roofed reader's platform whose position corresponded to that of the well in the mosque. The
congregation sat around the spacious courtyard in porticoes while the main ark was placed
in a niche in the wall where the mosque would
have had its *mihrab* (a niche in the direction of
Mecca, containing a copy of the Koran). The
most famous Hebrew Bible codex, known as
the Ben Asher codex and dating from the tenth
century, was deposited in this synagogue. In a

Praying in a synagogue in Sanaa, Yemen, c.1900.
(*Archive of Jewish Ethnography, Israel Museum,
Jerusalem/Photo: Hermann Burchardt*)

Worshippers after the Sabbath morning service in Sanaa,
1907.
(*The Jewish National and University Library,
Jerusalem/Photo: Hermann Burchardt*)

pogrom in 1947 this synagogue, along with the others in Aleppo, was burned to the ground, but the codex was rescued from the burning building by a member of the community and later smuggled to Israel.

Iraq, too, had ancient synagogues, some of them popularly ascribed to biblical figures who had lived there, such as Ezra and Daniel. In the twelfth century the ubiquitous Benjamin of Tudela came across a synagogue by the traditional grave of Ezekiel, next to the Euphrates River. It was the site of a popular pilgrimage for Jews from all over the country, made by the distinguished religious and secular leaders of the community during the Ten Days of Penitence, culminating in the reading of the book of Ezekiel on the Day of Atonement. Its reputation extended even to Moslems who also came to pray there.

In Baghdad Benjamin found twenty-eight synagogues, and when the Jews left Iraq in 1951 the number had grown to fifty-five. The Great Synagogue, where official ceremonies were held, was the most famous. Around its

walls were small compartments, each with a carpet-covered sofa for worshippers. The compartments and the ark, supported by twenty pillars, were covered, but the rest of the synagogue was open to the skies; across the top were beams on which covers could be laid in the event of rain. As in Talmudic times, Baghdad had 'summer' synagogues and 'winter' synagogues (in view of the heat only well-ventilated buildings could be used in summer).

In Yemen, at the southern end of the Arabian Peninsula, the Jews lived mostly in small villages, each with its synagogue. The nine thousand Jews of the capital city, Sanaa, had more than twenty-five synagogues in their quarter, some of them of considerable size. These were generally respected by the Moslem population, although there were periods of fanaticism when they were destroyed. In 1762, for example, the ruler, noticing that the town's fourteen synagogues were higher than its mosques, ordered them to be razed to the ground. They were soon rebuilt but three of them were adjudged insufficiently low, and consequently torn down. All synagogue ceilings were flat so as to avoid any possibility of mistaking them from the outside for mosques (which were vaulted). The buildings were generally square with windows on three sides (though not in the north, facing Jerusalem), and were barred from the outside against robbers. In addition to the windows, twelve holes were made in the walls – three in each, near the ceiling, corresponding to the twelve Tribes. On the stone walls between the windows were shelves for prayer-books and other sacred volumes. The ark took up almost the entire length of the northern wall and was divided by a shelf two-thirds of the way up, allowing for the larger scrolls to be placed below and the smaller ones above. Beneath the ark was the *geniza* for disused scrolls and holy books. The floor was not paved but whitewashed and covered with woollen rugs. No synagogue opened directly on to the street but had at least one, and sometimes two, courtyards, surrounded by a high wall and a locked entrance.

The reader's platform in the hall was close to the ark, usually resting on four wooden pillars and covered with precious embroidered cloths. A stand was provided for the translator, who, following Palestinian custom dating back to Second Temple times, translated the Torah reading, verse by verse, into Aramaic. Each worshipper brought two small cushions with him, one to sit on and the other to lean his back against. The Aden Synagogue received a donation from the Bombay philanthropist, David Sassoon, to purchase chairs for the worshippers, but the men continued to sit on the floor. The worshipper also brought a bench with him, but this too was not to sit on: it was where he placed his books during prayer and study. His sons would sit on the floor facing him from the other side of the bench and would read from their father's prayer-book, as a result of which young Yemenites learned to read upside down. Some congregants made a box out of the bench in which to keep their books and phylacteries, but they wore their prayer-shawl all day.

In neighbouring Arabia it was customary at an early period for Jews to pray five times a day in their synagogues, the three regular prayers, the *Shema* twice. This was probably the origin of the Moslem custom of praying five times daily.

In Palestine itself, the Jewish community of Jerusalem was massacred and burned in their synagogue by the Crusaders at the end of the eleventh century. When Benjamin of Tudela reached the country in *c*.1170 he found synagogues standing only in Ramleh and Tiberias. Another traveller, Samuel ben Samson, who visited there in 1210, reported twenty-four synagogues in Galilee and a number of beautiful ones in the Naveh and Irbid regions of Transjordan.

The Jerusalem community was re-established by the distinguished Spanish scholar, Nahmanides (or Ramban), who arrived in 1267. In a letter to his son he wrote: 'We found a ruined building with a beautiful dome supported by marble columns and we took it for a synagogue, for the city is ownerless and whoever wishes to take possession of some parts of the ruins may do so' (it is possible that the site he selected had, in fact, formerly been a synagogue). As described by another visitor, Obadiah of Bertinoro, some two centuries later, the Ramban Synagogue was a long, narrow and dark hall built on columns with light entering only through the door. In the middle a fountain played. Its large courtyard was fronted by many houses devoted to charitable purpose and inhabited by 'Ashkenazi widows'. In the sixteenth century it was still the town's sole synagogue, except for the small Karaite place of worship, which had been established about the same time. A Portuguese pilgrim wrote in 1560 that he was sad to see only one synagogue but that on festivals it took on a special lustre as it was decorated with precious golden curtains and exquisite silks sent by Jews all over the world. In 1586, however, the synagogue was confiscated. The sultan issued a firman in which he noted that when Saladin had taken Jerusalem four cen-

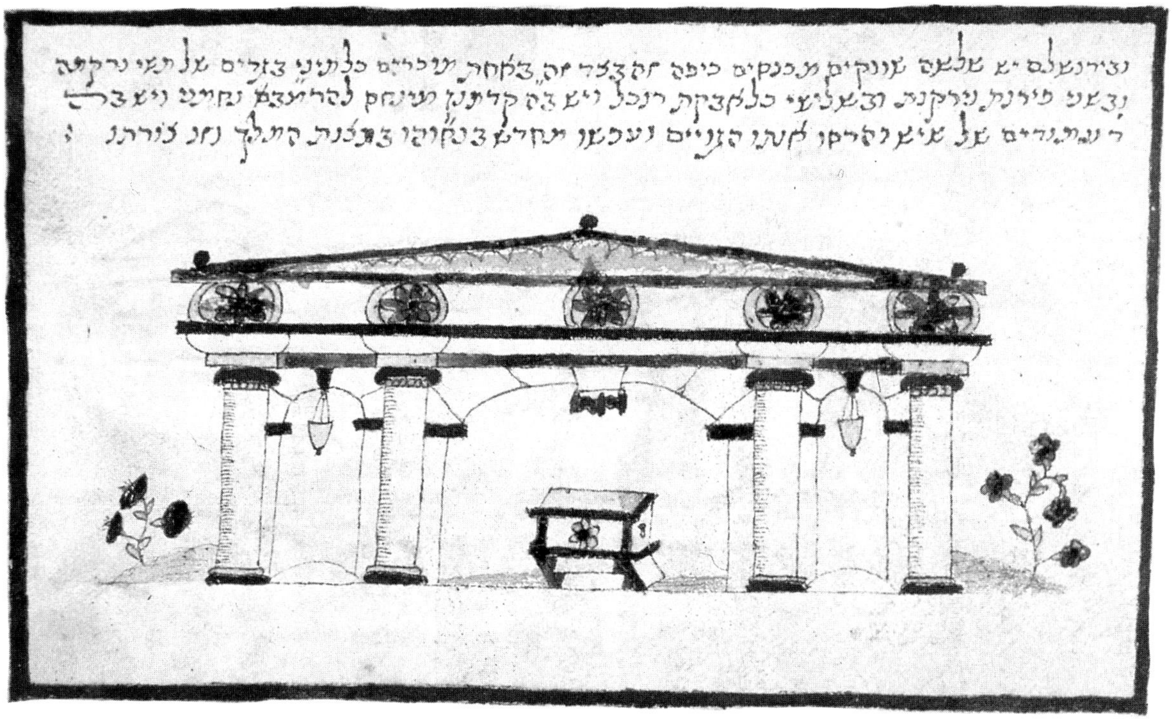

Ramban Synagogue in Jerusalem as depicted by the sixteenth-century 'Casale Pilgrim', who wrote in his dairy: 'In Jerusalem there is an ancient synagogue attributed to Rabbi Moses son of Nahman [Ramban]. In it are four pillars of marble. The gentiles destroyed it but it was recently rebuilt on orders of the ruler.' (C.Roth, 'The Casale Pilgrim', London, 1929)
(*Cecil Roth Collection*)

turies earlier there had been no synagogues, so the Jews had had no right to build one. Furthermore, it was next to a mosque and the Moslem worshippers were complaining that the 'noisy ceremonies' of the Jews were disturbing their devotions. He ordered that the mosque annex the Ramban Synagogue which was consequently turned into a warehouse.

Before long, however, the Ashkenazim living in Jerusalem built a new synagogue in the vicinity while Spanish refugees who had settled in Jerusalem constructed four synagogues within one complex. Although built within a few decades of each other, the four Sephardi synagogues are not of the same type. One feature they have in common is their sunken floor. Two of them (the Johanan ben Zakkai Synagogue and the small 'Middle' one) are single-naved while the other two (the Prophet Elijah and Istanbul Synagogues), betraying Turkish and Arab influence, are domed with a central space. These four synagogues, like all the others in the Old City, were destroyed by the Jordanians following the 1948 War, but after 1967 were restored (as was part of the Ramban synagogue) and are again in use. After the fifteenth century, synagogues in the country were as varied as the population. Apart from Jerusalem they were built in the three other 'holy cities', Hebron, Tiberias, and Safed. The revered domed Abraham Avinu Synagogue in Hebron, dating back to the sixteenth century, was destroyed in the Arab riots of 1929.

Towards the end of the sixteenth century the

sultan wrote from Turkey to the *qadi* (Moslem religious judge) of Damascus asking him to examine the proliferation of synagogues in Safed. 'The Jews who in olden times had three synagogues now have thirty-two and they have built them very high', he wrote. 'Furthermore, they have bought much property on which to build further synagogues' and this, he reports, had caused great annoyance to the Moslems. In the sixteenth century Safed had become a focus of Jewish mystical circles and at the beginning of the seventeenth century had twenty-one synagogues. Its two best-known synagogues were called after its greatest cabbalist, Rabbi Isaac Luria (the 'Ari'). The Sephardi 'Ari' Synagogue, the oldest and most interesting in Safed, is a single nave building with three arks in its southern wall and a high reader's platform dominating the hall. Originally there was no women's gallery, but in the rebuilding after the earthquake of 1837 one was introduced. The Ashkenazi 'Ari' Synagogue is a four-pillared structure in the East-European style,

with an ark the height of the hall, adorned with baroque wood carvings. The largest synagogue in Safed, the Isaac Aboab Synagogue, has three arks parallel to its three naves.

At the beginning of the eighteenth century the cabbalist, Judah Hasid, left the Ukraine for the Holy Land with 1,500 followers. He himself died a few days after his arrival and the impressive synagogue in Jerusalem started by his followers, but only completed at the end of the nineteenth century, was named after him (although it was better known as the 'Hurva', 'The Ruin', since it was originally constructed from a ruin). The 'Hurva' and the 'Tiferet Israel' (also named after its founder, Nissim Beck) Synagogues had high domes that seemed to reflect the domes of the great mosques on the Temple Mount and they towered above Jerusalem's Jewish Quarter, helping to impart its unique character. After 1948 both were among the fifty-eight synagogues destroyed by the Jordanians.

Left: Studying in the Johanan ben Zakkai Synagogue in Jerusalem, early twentieth century.
(*Central Zionist Archives, Jerusalem*)

Opposite, above left: The ark in the Ashkenazi 'Ari' Synagogue in Safed.
(*Photo: Amiram Harlap*)

Opposite, above right: Interior of the Isaac Aboab (Sephardi) Synagogue in Safed.
(*Ministry of Tourism, Jerusalem*)

Opposite, below: Hurva (or Judah Hasid) Synagogue in the Old City of Jerusalem. A noted landmark, it was considered the 'official' synagogue of the Jerusalem Jewish community.
(*Israel Museum, Jerusalem/Photo: Yaakov Ben-Dov*)

9

FAR-OFF PLACES

'DIASPORA' means dispersion, and the Jews found themselves dispersed throughout the world with communities in some of the most unlikely places. In many cases the origins of these communities are shrouded in legend and it cannot be established whether groups of Jews arrived and established themselves there or whether local inhabitants became infused with a love for Judaism which they proceeded to adopt. A number of these exotic communities were isolated and cut off from the mainstream of Jewish life for many centuries and developed their own customs and ceremonies. Their Jewish life revolved around the synagogue, with one exception – the Bene Israel of India, who lived along the Konkan coast, south of Bombay, and whose existence was not known to other Jews until the eighteenth century. They were known as 'Saturday oil pressers' because they did not work on Saturdays, and their Jewish observance was home-centred. Towards the end of the eighteenth century members of the Bene Israel began to move to Bombay, where they were introduced by other Jews (originating from Cochin in southern India and from Iraq) to aspects of traditional Judaism with which they were not familiar, including the synagogue.

They now began to build their own houses of worship, the first of which was opened in 1796. Its benefactor was Samuel Ezekiel Divekar, a Bene Israel soldier who had enlisted in the British Army in India and risen to command a battalion of the Bombay Native Infantry Regiment. He was captured by the notorious Tippu Sultan of Mysore, and according to one account, his release was secured by a group of Cochin Jews who took him to Cochin. There he was so impressed with their devotion to the synagogue that he vowed to build one in Bombay for the Bene Israel in thanksgiving for his rescue. The street in which this was built was named Samuel Street in his honour. He was its first president and, after his death in Cochin where he had gone to obtain Torah scrolls and other liturgical objects, the office remained in his family for the next century. By the mid-nineteenth century the original building had become too small and was demolished, and a new one was opened on the same site in 1860. On the centenary of the original building, in 1896, it was given the name Shaar Harahamim by which it is still known.

As the numbers of Bene Israel in Bombay grew, more synagogues were needed. A second one, popularly called the New Synagogue, was opened in 1841, and a third, Tifereth Israel, in the Jacob's Circle area of Bombay, in 1886. Ten years later, when bubonic plague struck the inner city, many Bene Israel moved out to the Jacob's Circle area and its synagogue became the most popular and richly decorated of all the

Knesseth Elijah Synagogue of the Iraqi Jews in Fort, Bombay, founded in 1888.
(*Beth Hatefutsoth Archive, Tel Aviv/Photo: Frederic Brenner*)

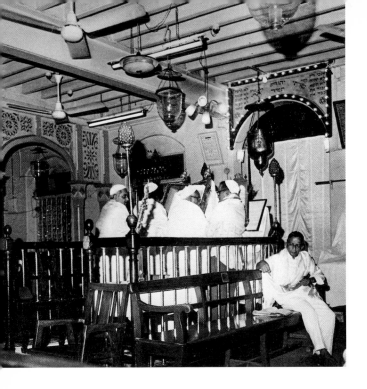

Above: Interior of the Tifereth Israel Synagogue, Bombay, built in 1886 and renovated in 1923. (*Photo: Carmel Berkson*)

Above: The sexton of the Magen Hasidim Synagogue lights an oil lamp inside the synagogue. (*Photo: Carmel Berkson*)

Below: Blowing the *shofar* on *Rosh Hashana* (New Year) in the Tifereth Israel Synagogue of the Bene Israel Jews, Bombay. (*Photo: Carmel Berkson*)

Below: Hazzan (reader) in the Magen Hasidim Synagogue, Bombay, seated on the platform. (*Photo: Carmel Berkson*)

Bene Israel places of worship. Another large synagogue, Magen Hasidim, was built in 1931; all the carpentry work on it was donated by Bene Israel. Before the large-scale emigration to Israel, the Bene Israel had more than twenty synagogues and prayer houses. One of these, Rodef Shalom, was a Reform congregation, the first in India, and was founded by an élite group who organized themselves into the 'Jewish Religious Union'.

The Bene Israel never produced a rabbi of their own. Individuals versed in the Bene Israel and Sephardi liturgy would act as readers and still do. Following Hindu and Moslem custom, the Bene Israel worshippers remove their shoes before entering the synagogue. They dress in bright colours to attend services except for the Day of Atonement, when they are clothed in white. The Jews must arrive in synagogue before dawn so as not to meet any non-Jews *en route*. Since travelling on public transport on the Sabbath was permitted in Bombay (and special coupons were used to avoid the handling of money), it was not necessary to attend a synagogue close to home and many would ride a considerable distance to services. They had no permanent synagogue seats and there was considerable mobility in synagogue affiliation. The synagogue became the centre of their community life and all family functions were conducted there. Every synagogue had arrangements so that the poor could sleep in the courtyard.

Once synagogues had been established in Bombay, the Jews who had remained on the Konkan coast also felt the need for houses of worship. The first was put up in 1840 in Alibag, which had become the British district administrative headquarters, and many Bene Israel moved there from their villages. The synagogue was rebuilt in 1910 with a charming garden where worshippers gathered on the

The exterior of the Magen Aboth Synagogue of the Bene Israel in Alibag on the Konkan coast. The first synagogue in the Konkan, it was built in the 1840s. (*Beth Hatefutsoth Archive, Tel Aviv/Photo: Frederic Brenner*)

Above: The interior of the Magen Aboth Synagogue, Alibag. The scrolls are kept under covers in polished wooden cases painted with flowers.
(*Photo: Carmel Berkson*)

Below: Bene Israel wedding ceremony in the Baghdadi synagogue, Magen David, Bombay. On her wedding day the bride wears a white sari and goes to greet the groom.
(*Photo: Carmel Berkson*)

Sabbath between the afternoon and evening services to read psalms. The sexton was provided with a bicycle to visit those congregants who still lived in the surrounding villages in order to keep them in touch with the community.

The other major Jewish group living in Bombay was of Iraqi origin. They maintained their own synagogues and for many years the Bene Israel were excluded from attending. Even when tension between the two groups abated, the two communities continued their separate existences. Calcutta was another large centre for Iraqi Jews and the first synagogue there was built in 1823. The largest and most imposing synagogue standing today is the Magen David, a red brick structure in a nineteenth-century Victorian pseudo-Renaissance style, dedicated in 1884 and modelled on the local Telegraph Office. Its 142-ft-high clock steeple towered over the heart of the city's commercial district. Ten years after it was dedicated, it adopted a set of rules enjoining decorum, of which a sample reads:

No one shall audibly felicitate fellow congregants as do the Arabic-speaking Jews who congratulate brides etc. with a shrill outcry. None shall throw sweets or flowers in the synagogue at any time. Confetti of any sort shall not be brought into the synagogue and the producing of any sound from any kind of instrument, even in the compound of the synagogue, is forbidden.

The behaviour of the congregation was so exemplary that when Hindu processions in the vicinity disturbed prayers, the police agreed to ban the playing of music within one hundred yards of the synagogue.

The main hall measured 92 ft × 33 ft and the stately ceiling was 50 ft high. The majestic effect was heightened by imposing granite pillars and stained-glass windows. The spacious

Magen David Synagogue in Calcutta, dedicated in 1884. (*Photo: Richard Loebell*)

ark, which was, in fact, a semicircular room, contained twenty scrolls, each housed in an elaborately decorated silver case. The Torah and ark covers were of precious materials, cashmere, velvet, or silk. There were special 'Haftara' scrolls used only to read the prophetical sections recited in the service. At one time the synagogue owned over a hundred scrolls, but most of them are now in other places where Calcutta Jews have settled.

There was no payment for synagogue seats in Calcutta and the main source of income came from auctioning prayer privileges. The auction was conducted in Arabic, although the purchaser marked his success with a blessing in Hebrew. In 1885 money was raised by raffling a scroll of the Law, and it was announced in the local paper as 'a holy lottery'. At its height, Calcutta Jewry had four synagogues, all of them usually crowded, but by the 1950s they were largely deserted, and daily services were conducted by 'minyan men', paid to attend.

Apart from the Bene Israel and the Iraqi Jews, the Jews of Cochin in the southern state of Kerala were another major Jewish community. In 1968 their main 'Paradesi' Synagogue was featured on an Indian stamp. The occasion was its four-hundredth anniversary, and its celebration was attended by people from all over the world. The Indian Prime Minister, Indira Gandhi, who spoke, ended her speech with the Hebrew greeting 'mazel tov' (which, she explained, she had learned from Fiddler on the Roof).

The Jews of Cochin were profoundly affected by the caste system. The original Jews who were of indeterminate origin were known as 'Black Jews' and were distinguished from the 'White Jews', who were later arrivals from Syria, Turkey, etc. A third group was composed of the 'Freedmen', Jews descended from converted native slaves. All 'White Jews' were members of the Paradesi Synagogue (i.e., 'the synagogue of the foreigners'). 'Black Jews' could pray there but were not eligible for membership and the 'Freedmen' had to sit on the floor or steps. There were seven other

The Paradesi Synagogue, Cochin (in the background) is next to the Hindu temple of the Rajah, whose grounds and palace adjoin the synagogue.
(*Photo: Richard Loebell*)

synagogues in the five Jewish settlements in Cochin and everyone belonged to the synagogue of his forefathers. In the event of 'intermarriage', the children would continue to pray in the paternal synagogue. The synagogues of the 'Black Jews' were reasonably affluent, although they lacked the fame and prestige of the Paradesi, and they were given rather confusing names: in the town of Ernakulam there was a 'Southside Synagogue' and a 'Riverside Synagogue', but the latter was on the south side of town where there was no river! The explanation for this was, however, simple:

clock descend as the clock unwinds itself. Each of the four sides of the tower has a clock face: one has Hebrew letters in place of numbers and is meant to be seen from the synagogue; one with Roman numerals faces the palace, for the benefit of the Raj; a third faces the Jewish Quarter (known as Jew Town); the fourth, with Indian numerals, is for the general public.

It was customary for the worshipper to remove his shoes – either because of the impact of local custom or to protect the white and blue hand-painted china-tiled floor with the famous willow pattern, each tile of a different design. According to one tradition, these tiles originally came from Canton in China and were meant to adorn the palace next door, but an astute Jew, who thought they would be a desirable adornment for the synagogue, persuaded the Hindu ruler that they were ritually unclean for Hindus as cows' blood had been used in their manufacture. The ruler was horrified and gratefully accepted the Jew's offer to remove them to the synagogue. (Most Cochinis today tend to discredit this story.)

An attractive feature of the synagogue is its colourful hanging oil lamps and crystal chandeliers. It has two reading desks: one used on weekdays in the centre of the hall, and the other, for the Sabbath and festivals. The latter is an extension of the women's gallery (which is separated from it by a lattice and reached by a stairway from the hall). The ark, superbly carved and ornamented in gold and red, contains a rich collection of scrolls. Three revered objects are kept in an antechamber. One is the Chair of Elijah, used at circumcision ceremonies when the entire congregation participates in placing it next to the western wall of the synagogue. It is covered with a long piece of damask and a Bible is placed upon it for the prophet Elijah to read from, if he makes his expected appearance. The second object is a table for family festivities in the synagogue. It holds bowls of water in which grapes have been soaked and sweet-smelling myrtle leaves to be distributed to all present. The third object is the laver for washing the hands of the priests

they were the names of the synagogues in another town, Cranganore, and Jews who moved from there to Ernakulam called their new places of worship by the names of their old synagogues.

The Paradesi Synagogue was built in the sixteenth century on land adjoining the royal palace which had been given to the Jews by the authorities. The original building was burned down by the Portuguese but soon replaced by the present one. One of its most prominent features is its Dutch-style tower, with a well at its foot, into which the weights of the tower

Opposite: The sixteenth-century Paradesi Synagogue in Cochin, India, the synagogue of the 'White' Jews of Middle Eastern origin. On each side of its Dutch-style tower is a clock, on one face of which the numbers are in Hebrew.
(Beth Hatefutsoth model/Photo: Michael Horton)

Above: Interior of the Paradesi Synagogue, Cochin.
(Beth Hatefutsoth model/Photo: Michael Horton)

before they give their blessing. The community's most precious possessions are the two copper plates received a thousand years ago, guaranteeing them their rights and privileges. They are kept in an iron box and jealously guarded by the elders.

The synagogue has never had a rabbi or a cantor and every person called to the reading of the Torah recites his own portion. Festivals are special highlights: on the eighth day of Tabernacles, for example, a six-year-old boy is called upon to make his 'début' in reading the prophetical portion. On the next day, the Rejoicing of the Law, the synagogue is bedecked with wreaths of jasmine and is alight with a myriad of candles. In front of the entrance is a pyramid of coconut lamps. The scrolls are removed from the ark and carried in procession outside the synagogue and around its outer circumference, along which a carpet has been laid. Each festival has its own colour scheme and the women's dresses and men's hats accord with this scheme: red and white for the New Year, white for the Day of Atonement, and green for Tabernacles. For the Rejoicing of the Law, however, a profusion of colours is the rule.

The most exotic of all synagogues stood east of India, in Kaifeng Fu, for centuries China's foremost cultural and commercial centre and seat of government. The community existed from the twelfth century but became known to the outside world only at the beginning of the seventeenth. The origin of the community is uncertain. They may have come from Persia but Yemen, India and Bokhara have also been suggested. They became indistinguishable from their fellow Chinese and at one time numbered several thousands, but by the time they were discovered they had dwindled to about a thousand.

News of the community stirred waves of excitement in Western Christian circles, who had long suspected that Jews had tampered with the scriptural text to tone down or eliminate Christological references. Now they hoped to examine long-preserved scrolls in

distant China far removed from the Christian orbit and from any temptation to change the text. They began to send missionaries, disguised as Chinese, to try and view the Scriptures, but the Jews were wary and wily and could not be persuaded to admit strangers into their synagogue. It was not until 1721 that a Christian gained admission, viewed the Hebrew scrolls, and discovered to his chagrin that they were identical to those in the West. It was with thanks to missionaries, however, that much of the information on this now-extinct community has been preserved. Italian Jesuits drew sketches of the synagogue in the early eighteenth century and Bishop William White, head of the Canadian Anglican Mission in Kaifeng, wrote the primary history of the community, whose Jewish practices – Sabbath, holidays, circumcision – were like those of the other Jews.

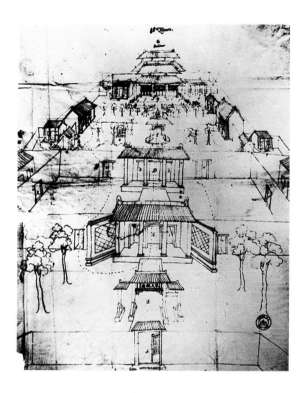

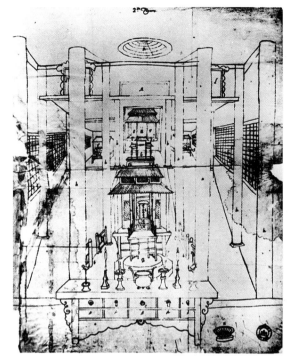

Above left: The courtyard of the Kaifeng Synagogue, drawn by the Jesuit missionary, Jean Domenge, in 1722. Entrance was through the east gate (1), then under the memorial arch (2) and then through the Great Gate into the first courtyard. A second gate led to the main courtyard, at the opposite end of which stood the synagogue.
(*Archives des Jesuites de Paris, Chantilly*)

Above right: Interior of the Kaifeng Synagogue, by Jean Domenge, 1722. In the foreground are a ceremonial table with a censer, flower vases, candlesticks and oil bowls. Beyond these is the chair of Moses, and behind this a canopy-covered table where the Emperor's tablet is displayed. At the far end stands the 'Bethel' or 'Ark of the Revered Scriptures'.
(*Archives des Jesuites de Paris, Chantilly*)

Opposite: Simhat Torah procession in Cochin, 1971. The scrolls are taken out of the synagogue and carried in procession around the grounds; the path is covered with a red carpet for the occasion.
(*Photo: Dan Kala*)

Right: A Kaifeng Jew reading from the Torah, placed on the chair of Moses, with two prompters. The man on the left holds a book with the Torah readings, written with vowels to help the reader. Drawing by Father Domenge, 1772.
(*Archives des Jesuites de Paris, Chantilly*)

Kaifeng Synagogue. The first synagogue of this community was built in 1163 and eventually surrounded by other communal structures. It was destroyed by a flood in 1461 and its replacement burned c.1600. A third synagogue was also washed away in a flood and the last synagogue was also washed away in a flood and the last until 1860. No pictures of the building are known, but Italian Jesuits made drawings of the pagoda-like building in the eighteenth century and it is on the basis of these that Beth Hatefutsoth made its reconstruction. (*Beth Hatefutsoth model/Photo: Michael Horton*)

Entrance to the street in Kaifeng which led to the synagogue, 1924. Its Chinese name means 'The Lane of the Sect which teaches the Scriptures'.
(*Beth Hatefutsoth Archive, Tel Aviv/Photo: Alexander Horne*)

Rubbings taken in 1946 from the inscription on the memorial stone which once stood in the Kaifeng Synagogue courtyard and is now in the Kaifeng Museum. The inscription on the left tells the story of the Jews of Kaifeng, from the days of the patriarch Abraham; that on the right includes a description of Jewish customs.
(*Yad Ben-Zvi, Jerusalem*)

Several synagogues had stood on the same site, at the intersection of Earth-Market Character Street and Fire-God Shrine Street, the first being built in 1163. But as the result of fire and flood, they were frequently destroyed – and they were always rebuilt. The proximity to the Yellow River made the area particularly susceptible to inundation and in the big flood of 1642 the synagogue was destroyed and the Torah scrolls washed away. They were eventually rescued, however, dried, patiently restored and returned to use. By the nineteenth century, though, there was no longer anyone who could read them. A pathetic notice displayed in the market square sought any traveller who might be able to read Hebrew, but in vain.

The last synagogue built on this spot was dedicated in 1663. It had a pagoda-like exterior with a three-tiered roof and Chinese furnishings but still retained a strong Jewish atmosphere. It occupied a spacious plot (400 ft × 150 ft) and entrance was from an alley named in its honour: Lane of the Pluck-Sinew Religion (which was how the local population called Judaism, after its method of preparing meat). The orientation was towards Jerusalem in the west, and over the entrance the description 'Temple of Purity and Truth' was written in Chinese. Access to the synagogue was through three courtyards, which included ornamental archways, an open terrace for a *sukka* (booth for the Feast of Tabernacles), two stone monuments giving information on the history of the community, and buildings along the sides used as residences, a study hall, a ritual bath, and a recess for slaughtering animals. Worshippers were summoned to services by the sounding of a jade chime and before entering the synagogue removed their shoes. Inside the synagogue the worshipper first encountered a table on which were placed the five ceremonial objects found in Chinese temples: a censer, two vases of flowers, two candlesticks, and two oil bowls. Beyond the table was the Throne of Moses on which the Torah scroll was placed for its weekly reading and above it the *Shema* was inscribed in letters of gold. In the western wall stood the ark, containing thirteen scrolls, each in its own case, and above the ark an inscription promising obedience to the emperor – a mandatory feature of all Chinese places of worship. On one side of the synagogue was the 'hall of the ancestors', obviously derived from Confucianism. Here there were incense bowls dedicated to the Jewish patriarchs, to the ancestors of the community – and to Confucius!

Around the synagogue and in the grounds were tablets whose inscriptions reveal a Jewish-Confucian syncretism. One of them reads: 'The Confucian religion and Judaism agree on all essential points and only differ on secondary issues.' Men and women sat separately and the men wore blue caps (to distinguish them from Moslems who wore white caps at prayer). The face of the Torah reader was covered with a veil, a custom induced, perhaps, by the Bible story of Moses who did this when giving the Torah to the people (Exodus 34:31–5). Animal sacrifice to the ancestors was practised until a late date.

From the seventeenth century onwards, in the absence of trained spiritual leaders, the community deteriorated. Communal life ended in the nineteenth century when the synagogue crumbled into a state of complete disrepair and no means were available for its restoration. Eventually (*c.*1860) it was demolished. The site became covered with mire and was sold to Canadian missionaries. Some of its contents have, none the less, been preserved – in a local mosque, in a Confucian temple and museum, and in museums in England, Austria, the United States, and Canada.

There was still another Jewish community long unknown to the western world living in the heart of Africa – in Ethiopia. Long known as 'Falashas', the term (meaning 'exiles') is now considered pejorative and they are more usually referred to today by the name they call themselves – Beta Israel ('House of Israel'). Their origin must be left to speculation but they have existed from very early times and often had to fight for their very survival against the dominant Christians. They eventually concentrated in the Gondar province, living in small remote villages where they tenaciously clung to their religion. There they were discovered by westerners only in the nineteenth century. In 1862 a missionary, Henry A. Stern, published an account of their worship:

Their places of worship, like the Christian churches in the country, consist of three divisions, with an entrance towards the east. Admission into these different courts is rigorously regulated by the Levitical law, and the severest penalty would be inflicted on anyone who should incautiously pollute the sacred edifice. In the rear of every place of worship is a small enclosure with a huge stone in the centre; and on this crude altar the victim is slaughtered and all other sacrificial rites performed. Their sacrifices are most capriciously offered and – with the exception of the paschal lamb – neither the offering on the Sabbath nor on the Day of Atonement is in accordance with the original command ... Saturday after Saturday, the Falasha congregations throughout Abyssinia [Ethiopia] hear in their places of worship a discourse on the edifying topic of the laws of purification; even a stranger is condemned to listen amidst the melodious *la la la*'s of the women to a chapter describing leprosy, plague or other ills which sin and dirt, vice and ungodliness have entailed on offending humanity.

Stern writes that on Saturday mornings 'knots of figures enveloped in the graceful folds of a white cotton dress troop over the green sward to the humble building dedicated to the service of God'. Stern's description would be equally applicable today. Every village had its synagogue (called *masgid*, a word which resembles the Arabic for mosque, *misgad*), with at least one resident priest (who, in the absence of a rabbi, served as the religious leader). The *masgid* might be inside or outside the village and resembled the straw-thatched huts in which the community lived, except that it was perhaps larger, had two or four entrances, and was sometimes marked by a Star of David. A unique feature of Ethiopian Judaism was the fact that it had an order of monks, an institution derived from the Christian environment. The monks were endowed with special sanctity and the eastern entrance to the synagogue was reserved for them (in which case the lay worshippers would enter from the west). On entering, they would face toward Jerusalem and prostrate themselves.

The humble synagogues were influenced in their design by the surrounding churches. The outer area was for laymen, while the inner section, or Holy of Holies, could be entered only by priests and monks. The scroll of the Law and the priests' ceremonial vestments were kept here. When only one room was available, the scroll of the Law was placed on a high decorated board on the eastern wall or suspended from the ceiling. In some places, however, it was kept in the home of the priest along with other sacred objects including the sacrificial knife and ceremonial umbrellas (the Jewish priests, like their Christian counterparts, unfurled these umbrellas on special ritual occasions). The priests were provided with benches in the synagogue for resting after the performance of their duties but no other seating was introduced. No separate section was allotted to the women and only unmarried girls and elderly women were allowed to enter; the others had to remain outside. Persons in a state of ritual impurity and non-Jews were not permitted inside.

The priests prayed six times during the day and four times at night but the congregants attended a maximum of two such services, one in the morning and one in the evening. The main attendance was on the Sabbath and festivals. The language of the Bible was the ancient tongue of Ge'ez which was understood only by the priests who translated the readings into the vernacular for the congregation. The priest usually recited the service by heart but on

Above: Inside the synagogue at Shewata, Ethiopia, on the Sabbath, 1983. The Sabbath loaves are in the baskets. (*Beth Hatefutsoth Archive, Tel Aviv/Photo: Frederic Brenner*)

Below: Priests in front of the synagogue at Gajna, Ethiopia, 1937. (*Photo: Carlo Alberto Viterbo*)

the Sabbath and festivals he could use a prayer-book which had to be written on parchment, not paper. Formerly, the entire congregation covered their heads in the synagogue but in time this was restricted to the priests. Occasionally, during the service, the priests would strike a drum or gong, and for special festivals they would sprinkle grain and herbs on the synagogue floor to ensure a pleasant fragrance. The synagogue was unique in that it had a sacrificial altar because sacrifice was not practised by the Christians. In the last century the use of sacrifice became increasingly restricted among the Jews and was eventually confined to the Passover lamb. By the 1960s this, too, was abandoned.

In recent years the bulk of Ethiopian Jewry have emigrated to Israel, and they are being influenced by the synagogue styles of their new neighbours. Those who have remained, most of them elderly, continue to follow their ancient traditions.

Right, above: An Ethiopian community outside their synagogue (characterized by the Shield of David on its roof) on the Day of Atonement.
(*Courtesy of Yona Bogale, Petach-Tikva*)

Right, centre: Priests in traditional garb at the synagogue in the Ethiopian village of Walaka, 1984.
(*Beth Hatefutsoth Archive, Tel Aviv/Photo: Doron Bacher*)

Right, below: The priests leaving the synagogue to distribute the Sabbath loaves after the Sabbath service. The men and women wait separately on either side of the entrance. Shewata, Ethiopia, 1983.
(*Beth Hatefutsoth Archive, Tel Aviv/Photo: Frederic Brenner*)

10

EQUAL CITIZENS

DURING the Age of enlightenment and Emancipation the many discriminatory practices against the Jews which had been imposed in Christian countries over a period of fifteen centuries were redressed. It was a process which spread gradually from West to East, first in the wake of the American and French Revolutions. In Europe the message of equality was brought by Napoleon's armies to western and central Europe (although in many of these countries it was not finally achieved until the second half of the nineteenth century). For the Jewish masses in the Russian Empire (which included Poland and the Baltic countries) full civil rights were achieved only in 1917.

The Jews now emerged from their isolation to enter society as equal citizens. The impact of the majority culture was powerful and Jews came face to face with the enticement of assimilation. Moreover, as a result of Napoleon's initiative, the whole concept of the Jewish 'community' underwent a fundamental change. It was no longer recognized as a separate community but only as a religious entity, and membership was now voluntary: if they so chose, Jews could opt out.

Emancipated Jews were caught between their desire to resemble their non-Jewish neighbours and prove themselves loyal citizens of the countries where they lived, and the determination to continue to assert their Jewishness. This ambivalence was reflected in synagogue buildings and activities. In France and Belgium Napoleon had organized the official Jewish bodies into 'consistories' whose functions were solely religious. One indication of the changes to come was the governmental regulation ordering rabbis to dress in a similar fashion to Christian clerics. (In England such costume was adopted voluntarily.) In France small prayer-houses were closed down and worship concentrated in the formal synagogues. The first important building of this kind in Paris opened in 1822, and was called the 'Temple of rue Notre-Dame-de-Nazareth', a name which smacks of assimilation. It was an impressive neo-Classical edifice resembling a Roman basilica. The consistories built large synagogues in other major Jewish centres including many in places where none had previously existed. The process was facilitated by the Jews' newly-won right to own land and the right of the consistories to impose and collect taxes for religious purposes. Moreover, like the churches, the synagogues now enjoyed the right to request government subsidies.

The main building activity went on in Germany, where a number of distinguished

---

Oranienburgerstrasse Synagogue in Berlin, built in 1866 in the Oriental style. At the time, it was the largest synagogue in the world and a pioneer in its use of gas lighting. Unlike earlier synagogues, whose exteriors were as inconspicuous as possible, this was a landmark, on a main thoroughfare. It was severely damaged on Crystal Night, 1938, and the remains were destroyed in the Allied bombing of Berlin during the Second World War. (*Landesbildstette, Berlin*)

synagogues had already been built in the eighteenth century. In Frankfurt, where the Judenstrasse (Jews' Street) had been burned down in 1711, the replacement included a fine synagogue hall with a three-storey women's annexe, with small windows opening on to the prayer hall. As Germany's rulers came under the influence of the Enlightenment, their attitudes to Jews and Jewish places of worship became sympathetic. King Frederick William I of Prussia permitted the new Jewish community in Berlin to build the Heidereutergasse Synagogue which was dedicated in 1714 in the presence of the monarch. The ruler of Ansbach took the initiative in proposing the erection of a communal synagogue which was opened in 1746 (and was one of the few German synagogues, and probably the oldest, to survive the Holocaust). The Munich Synagogue was dedicated in 1826 in the presence of King Ludwig I of Bavaria who had contributed to its establishment.

During the nineteenth century over two hundred large and lavish synagogues were built in Germany. The various legal restrictions on their construction were gradually abolished and the way opened for the integration of the synagogues into their surroundings. Unlike the modest synagogues of previous ages, secluded in the narrow confines of the Jewish quarter, the new synagogues were monumental. The architects stressed the façade, usually opening on to a major thoroughfare, and even added imposing exteriors and entrances on the other sides. The Jews discovered that their neigh-

Left, above: Interior of Frankfurt Synagogue, built on the site of the earlier synagogue in the Judenstrasse and incorporating many of the features of the earlier building.
(*Beth Hatefutsoth Archive, Tel Aviv/Photo: Dr Paul Arnsberg Collection*)

Left, below: The Heidereutergasse Synagogue, the first community synagogue in Berlin. The masonry building is in a Protestant baroque style with an impressive ark framed with columns. The large reader's desk occupied the centre of the hall. The synagogue was badly damaged in the bombing of Berlin during the Second World War.
(*R. Krautheimer, 'Mittelalterliche Synagogen', Berlin, 1927*)

bours' churches were endowed with great appeal through the beauty of their form, the effect of subdued lighting, and the aesthetic use of music (which required proper acoustics), and they employed these principles in their synagogues. The Jews were now moving into the large cities and wanted to make their presence known through a combination of harmonious integration into the environment and an expression of Jewish uniqueness.

The emergence of the Reform movement in Judaism – intended to appeal to Jews attracted by the general culture, including Christianity, and who were in danger of becoming lost to Judaism – proved to have a major influence on synagogue design. The Reform Jews stressed the universal teachings of Judaism while their revised liturgy and the aesthetic appeal of the synagogue and its services aimed at providing a religious experience that would allure and satisfy those who were disillusioned with Orthodoxy. The first such modern synagogue was opened in Seesen in Central Germany in 1810. It was called a 'temple', in imitation of the term used in France for the new places of worship. There was another reason too. The Reform Jews held that the Jewish people were not in exile and considered every house of worship a temple, as holy as the original Temple in Jerusalem. The moving spirit in Seesen was Israel Jacobson, who has been called the 'father of Reform Judaism'. A contemporary account of the dedication of this 'Temple of Jacob' indicates its innovative spirit:

On the day of the dedication, lovely music re-sounded from the roof of the temple and announced to the city the approaching festivities. The assembly included persons of distinguished rank, scholars, Jewish, Protestant, and Catholic clergymen, businessmen of all kinds, all walking together in complete concord. Uniform tolerance seemed to permeate all. At 9.00 the ringing of bells announced that the ceremonies would begin and the procession proceeded from the hall into the temple. There came from the organ loft lovely music by sixty musicians and singers. After everyone had taken their seats, a cantata specially composed for this celebration was sung.[1]

The ritual further included readings from the Bible in Hebrew and German, a chorale for choir and organ sung first in Hebrew and then in German, and addresses by Jacobson and by a church counsellor. In his remarks Jacobson, while asserting his adherence to the faith of his fathers, stressed that progressive enlightenment depended on a rapprochement with Christian neighbours. 'Who would dare to deny', he asked, 'that our service is sickly because of many useless things and that it has in part degenerated into a thoughtless recitation of prayers and formulae that kills devotion more than it encourages it? Our ritual is weighted down with religious customs which must be rightfully offensive to reason as well as to our Christian friends.'

Systematic reform of the service began a few years later in Hamburg and was initially limited to prayers and a sermon in German, choral singing and organ music. But gradually other changes were introduced. The Hungarian rabbi, Aaron Chorin, was the first to permit prayer with uncovered head as well as travelling on the Sabbath under certain conditions (which meant that Jews did not have to live in the proximity of a synagogue). The introduction of an organ gave rise to bitter controversy. The Orthodox authority, Moses Sofer of Pressburg in Hungary, forbade it – even if played by a non-Jew. First of all, it was a 'pagan' instrument and, secondly, ever since the destruction of the Second Temple, the rabbis had banished joy from the service, and this included the playing of any musical instrument. The Reform Jews replied that if vocal music was permitted, instrumental music should also be allowed. Furthermore, the so-called pagans (i.e., the Christians) had derived the use of the organ from the Temple in Jerusalem.

One major change in synagogue design resulting from the Reform movement was the positioning of the reader's desk so that it merged with the platform in front of the ark. It was often no more than a marble table. This cleared the central space for extra seating

The inscription on the building reads: וְעָשׂוּ לִי מִקְדָּשׁ וְשָׁכַנְתִּי בְּתוֹכָם

Above: The Great Synagogue in Stockholm, a large brick building erected in 1870 and still in use. The inscription above the entrance reads: 'Let them make me a sanctuary that I may dwell among them.' (Exodus 25:8)
(Beth Hatefutsoth Archive, Tel Aviv/Courtesy of Yakov Kaplan, Tel Aviv)

Opposite: Praying in the Dohany Street Synagogue, Budapest, completed in 1859 and still in use. This hall, which has a double gallery for women, can hold three thousand worshippers.
(Photo: Hegyi Gabor)

which was now arranged in long rows facing the ark. Men and women sat together in family pews which replaced the old movable desks. As the function of the synagogue was now solely religious and no longer communal, the platform lost its centrality and attention was concentrated on the lavishly-designed ark (which did not necessarily face Jerusalem). Provision had to be made for organ and choir, usually over the ark or at the back of the hall. The added importance of the sermon led to emphasis on the pulpit or lectern, usually in front of the ark but sometimes, following church precedents, at the side. The women's annexe was now unnecessary and the incorporation of a gallery was optional. The new arrangements aroused the opposition of Orthodox authorities who felt that they were direct imitations of churches. Except with regard to mixed seating, however, opposition was not on principle. Orthodox authorities from the past were cited who had ruled that it was not obligatory to place the platform in the centre of the hall. In the course of time, Orthodox synagogues were built along similar lines and introduced choral singing and sermons in the vernacular. The interior architecture of the synagogue was now more assimilable to church design and in the United States, for example, churches were often bought and converted into synagogues with few problems of adaptation. The Reform temples maintained a strict decorum, derived more from the example of the church than the synagogue. Many prayers were recited in unison by the congregation in place of the

Orthodox tradition of individual recitation, condemned by the Reform as an undignified Babel. Other innovations included robing rooms for the officials, who now wore canonicals, and a study for the rabbi. The forecourt became a spacious lobby.

The synagogues of the nineteenth century were built in a bewildering variety of imitative styles, inspired by architecture from earlier periods and distant realms. These styles were often artificially derived and eclectically applied, sometimes with little co-ordination between the exterior and the interior. In the early part of the century the architects were all Christians who imposed their own approaches and traditions.

Following the French Revolution, neo-Classicism was the favoured style among architects of churches and synagogues, all of which were grandiosely called 'temples'. The growing interest in Greek and Roman archaeology was reflected in many of the details. A synagogue built at Woerlitz in 1790, by the court architect of the Duke of Anhalt-Dessau, was a round pavilion also known as the Temple of Vesta, inspired by ancient temples to this Roman goddess. The synagogue at Alt-Ofen (now part of Budapest), opened in 1820, looked like a classical temple from the outside while in its hall the reader's desk was enclosed by four obelisks topped by eagles carrying globes. The early large synagogues in the big cities were also in the neo-Classical style, such as Vienna's Seitenstettengasse Temple, built in 1826, whose design may have been influenced by the Pantheon in Rome.

The desire of Jews to assert their individuality and to find original and distinguishing features led to their widespread use of oriental motifs. The Orient had caught the imagination of Europeans ever since Napoleon's Egyptian expedition of 1798, and became fashionable in many decorative contexts. The Jews garnered sufficient self-confidence to make a public

Opposite: The Seitenstettengasse Synagogue in Vienna, dedicated in 1826. The oval hall contained twelve columns supporting two tiers of galleries.
(*Courtesy of Professor Kurt Schubert, Vienna*)

Right: Synagogue in Obuda, Budapest, built 1820–1. This neo-Classical building, with a clock in its façade, was considered the outstanding synagogue in the Hapsburg Empire in the early nineteenth century. It is no longer used as a synagogue.
(*Magyar Munkasmozgalmi Museum, Budapest*)

Below: Exterior of the Great Synagogue, Tlomacka Street, Warsaw, consecrated in 1878 in the presence of the Governor General of Poland. Its colonnaded portico with flanking pavilions and high Oriental dome made it an outstanding building in the city. It was blown up by the Germans in 1943.
(*Beth Hatefutsoth Archive, Tel Aviv*)

Above: Dohany Street Synagogue, Budapest. Its bulbous gilded cupolas reflect Islamic motifs. The building to the left, added later, is the birthplace of Theodor Herzl (who celebrated his barmitzvah in the synagogue) and now houses a Hungarian Jewish Museum.
(*Yad Vashem Archives, Jerusalem*)

Below: Interior of the Tiempo Israelitico, Florence, showing the strong Oriental influence in the ornamentation, including multicoloured mosaics and tiles. The ark stands in an apse and the reader's desk is in an enclosed area in the centre. On the left is the pulpit, attached to the northern wall.
(*Beth Hatefutsoth Archive, Tel Aviv*)

statement affirming their oriental origins. It was also widely believed that Solomon's Temple must have looked like its Egyptian counterparts. Nineteenth-century European synagogues incorporated, therefore, a variety of Egyptian, Byzantine, and Moorish styles and elements – often side by side with the neo-Classical, the neo-Gothic, and the Romanesque.

An outstanding synagogue in the oriental style was built in Dresden, in 1838–40, behind a sedate conventional Romanesque exterior. Its lavish interior incorporated Byzantine forms and ornamentation inspired by Moorish (or Saracenic) sources, such as the Alhambra in Granada. It set the tone for many other synagogues utilizing oriental, or neo-Islamic, motifs. This was expressed externally through large cupolas, onion-shaped or bulbous domes, minaret-like turrets, horseshoe arches, and mosaic decorations. Interiors were decorated with rich floral and geometrical patterns. The oriental style suited the desire of Jews for affluent buildings while the abstract ornamentation was considered appropriate for synagogues since even the Reform temples tended to avoid representational art. The Orthodox Jews liked it because it was so different from church architecture that there could be no suspicion of imitation. Sephardim were attracted because it reminded them of their origins, while at the end of the century it was endorsed in Zionist circles because it pointed to their destiny. The oriental elements were not copied slavishly but were appropriately blended with traditional elements of European architecture in general and synagogue architecture in particular. The Leipzig Synagogue, inaugurated in 1858, became particularly influential as Jews attending the famous Leipzig fairs were impressed by its mosque-like features. One of the most distinguished examples was dedicated in Florence in 1882. Its builders derived their designs from Byzantine, Islamic and Spanish Moorish sources. Its basic plan was inspired by Santa Sofia in Istanbul and its massive dome, prominent even in Florence, by Egyptian examples.

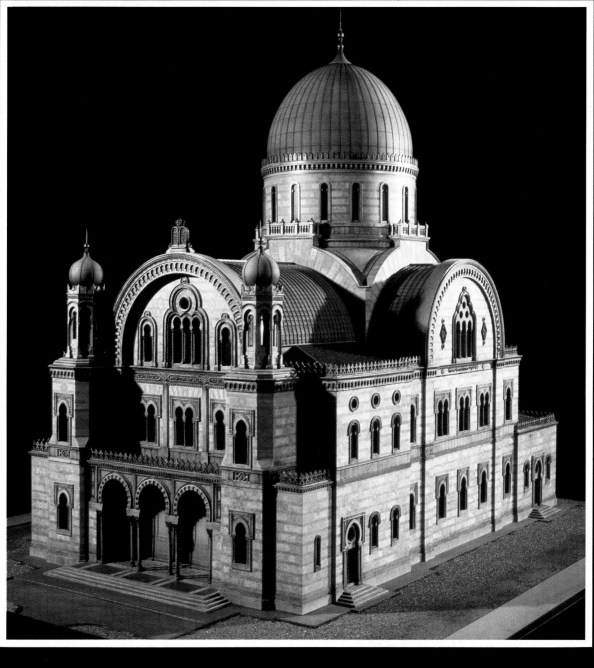

Exterior of the Florence synagogue, Tiempo Israelitico,

Above: Interior of the Oranienburgerstrasse Synagogue in Berlin. The apse, as wide as the nave, contained not only the ark but also had space for the choir and organ. The hall held 3,000 worshippers, including 1,200 women in the galleries. The reader's desk was next to the ark. This was regarded as one of the richest and most fashionable synagogues of its day.
(*Courtesy of Dr Edna Meyer, Tel Aviv*)

Opposite, above: Kassel Synagogue, built in 1836–9, whose combinations of Classical and Romanesque styles widely influenced subsequent synagogue architecture. The entrance, in the centre of the façade, is under a three-cornered gable surmounted by the Tablets of the Law. The 'round arch' style, characteristic of the period, defines its exterior. The building was destroyed by the Nazis.
(*Engraving designed by I.Robbock/Stadtarchiv, Kassel*)

Not all Jews, however, were happy with the individuality of the oriental styles. Some preferred models taken from general European architecture, in particular the Romanesque style of the early Middle Ages, regarded as eminently 'German'. To quote Edwin Oppler, one of the leading Jewish synagogue architects, 'The German Jew living in a German state should build in a German style'. For these Jews synagogues in the Romanesque style were still distinguishable from churches, but at least proclaimed the users as Europeans and not as exotic easterners. Even the Jews in Algiers built a neo-Romanesque synagogue to proclaim their difference from the Moslems and their identification with the European rulers.

The 'mother' synagogue in this style was built in Kassel in 1834–9 with a Romanesque exterior although its interior betrayed other influences. In 1862–70 Oppler built the synagogue in Hanover of which he wrote 'The building, which is in an open space and near a church, represents a triumph for nineteenth-century Jewry. A generation hence they will point to these buildings and say "See what an effort our fathers were prepared to make to erect a monument to God"'. Generally, the neo-Gothic style was not favoured since it was too closely associated with churches and cathedrals, but it did make its mark in some synagogues (largely under the influence of the Prague Altneuschul). The three synagogues in Vienna and the remodelled Maisl Synagogue in Prague were examples of this. To Oppler, however, there was an important difference from Christian places of worship in all these structures: 'Synagogues are distinguished from churches in their ground plan which avoids the shape of the cross.'

The synagogues of this period introduced a change in favoured symbols. The familiar symbols, such as the seven-branched candelabrum (*menora*), the ram's horn (*shofar*), and the four species associated with the Feast of Tabernacles, fell out of favour, perhaps because their connection with the Jerusalem Temple evoked a suggestion of 'exile' and perhaps the hope for 'Redemption', concepts that seemed counter to universalism, rationalism, and loyalty to one's native land. Their place was taken by two symbols: the hexagonal Star of David (*Magen David*), an ancient magical symbol recently adopted by the Jews, and the Tablets of the Law which proclaimed the theological-ethical message of the Jews which had been assimilated and appreciated by Christianity. These symbols projected the antiquity and morality of Jewish culture which was the image preferred by the Jews. The two symbols were prominently displayed on synagogue exteriors (often on locations corresponding to the cross on churches) and were incorporated into the design of windows and gables and, in various ingenious fashions, into the interior design.

During the nineteenth century synagogue building became recognized as a specialized branch of architecture. Tenders put out by

Below: The synagogue on Petersburg Place, Bayswater, London, built in the second half of the nineteenth century. Engraving.
(*Beth Hatefutsoth Archive, Tel Aviv*)

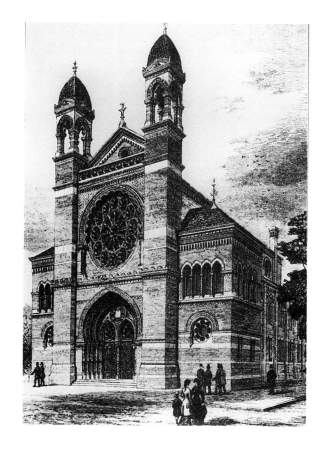

Opposite, above: Romanesque-style Roonstrasse Synagogue in Cologne, 1899.
(*Rheinisches Bildarchiv, Cologne*)

Opposite, below: Triple-domed Fasanenstrasse Temple in Berlin, built in 1912 and burned down by the Nazis in 1938.
(*Landesbildstelle, Berlin*)

Right: Romanesque synagogue in Kaliningrad, Russia, formerly Königsberg, capital of East Prussia. It was burned down on Crystal Night, 1938.
(*Beth Hatefutsoth Archive, Tel Aviv*)

Below: The Great Synagogue in Sydney, Australia, built in 1878 and still in use.
(*Keter Publishing House, Jerusalem*)

Jewish communities received proposals by the leading architects of the time. The professional journals regularly reported on developments in synagogue building, sometimes accompanied by theoretical controversies. From the middle of the century Jews gradually entered the profession, and congregations would often turn to Jewish architects, such as Oppler and Albert Rosengarten in Germany, or George Basevi and David Mocatta (who was best known as a designer of railroad stations), in England.

With the turn of the twentieth century synagogues were influenced by modern styles of architecture and by new materials such as cast iron and artificial stone. They were more conservative, less florid and exotic. Again, German Jews were the vanguard of these developments. One of the first of the twentieth-century synagogues was in Potsdam, seat of the Kaiser, who took a personal interest in the building and even rejected the first design submitted to him as not sufficiently worthy of its environment. The Essen Synagogue, dedicated in 1914, was particularly ambitious, its functional design reflecting innovative architectural and artistic trends. Its bronze doors, stained-glass windows (which had become increasingly accepted despite the objections of some rabbis who condemned them as an imitation of church usage), and mosaic medallions on the walls and ceiling displayed a variety of Jewish symbols, drawing on the usage of recently excavated ancient Galilean synagogues. An Art Nouveau synagogue was erected in rue Pavée in Paris, in 1913, built by an Orthodox congregation of eastern European immigrants. Although these newcomers had little contact with western aesthetics, they built an attractive synagogue of great originality and pioneering modernity.

A vivid picture of Friday evening worship at the main Paris synagogue in the rue de la Victoire (built in 1874) is given by the English Jewish writer, Israel Cohen, in his *Travels in Jewry*:

To my surprise, I found a concourse of men and women streaming into the house of prayer. In the spacious and lofty vestibule, a beadle with the cocked hat of an admiral and the resplendent chain of a mayor paced to and fro with a charity box which he offered to each arrival, a sign that here at least you were not expected to observe the orthodox rule of leaving your purse at home when going to meet the Sabbath bride.

Within, the synagogue, vast and lofty, presents a scene of ornate and overwhelming grandeur; with its tall marble pillars, its galleries with vaulted arches, its celestial cupola, its stained-glass rose-windows, and the brilliant illumination of its

towering multi-branched candelabra, it is suggestive, both in the magnitude of its proportions and the beauty of its design, of a cathedral, but is free from the all-pervading gloom that depresses the interior of so many minsters. An enormous dais at the upper end, approached by a series of steps, is occupied by the reader's platform, and on a higher level, with the Ark of the Law, sit the Chief Rabbi of Paris and an assistant Rabbi and on the right, in solitary dignity, the Chief Rabbi of France with the red ribbon of the Legion of Honour. All three wear round, flattish hats like French priests. In the congregation were more than a thousand people, the men occupying all the middle benches and the women, dressed mostly in black, filling the galleries on either side. The decorum was beyond reproach.

The service was intoned by a cantor, responses coming from a choir perched in a lofty gallery facing the Ark, but most of the congregation seemed content to leave the praying to the tuneful precentor. The sermon was delivered by a rabbi from the lectern at the side of the reader's platform. His sermon dealt with the rebuilding of the Temple ... It might have been a sermon in the seventeenth century or even the seventh. For this Rabbi apparently nothing had happened since the downfall of Judea. I wondered whether such a jejune discourse could secure the attachment of his flock or evoke in their breast even an ephemeral response.

The developments in nineteenth-century Europe were paralleled in the United States where the small Jewish community at the beginning of the century expanded rapidly – first thanks to immigration from central Europe which determined the nature of its communal life, and then with the arrival of newcomers from eastern Europe, culminating in the mass influx which started in the early 1880s when Jewish life, including education and philanthropy, was synagogue-centred; but from 1813 other organizations began to be formed which were to compete with the synagogue.

The Ashkenazim, now outnumbering the Sephardim, broke away to establish their own congregations, although this did not mean any major change in synagogue structure as both groups had a similar concept of the function of the synagogue. The comprehensive role of the institution ended as a result of both geographic decentralization and new outlooks, religious and secular, which fragmented American Jewry. The diversity was expressed in splits between Orthodoxy and Reform, old-established Jews and newcomers from a variety of origins as well as the new areas of settlement stretching from coast to coast. Synagogues proliferated throughout the country, many of them independent and establishing their own customs. With the emergence of community organizations the role of the synagogue was no

Opposite, far left: Synagogue in Essen, 1914. At the time of its construction it was widely praised for its modernity and originality. Approach was through a forecourt and, after climbing a broad stairway, the worshipper entered a spacious lobby leading to the hall of worship.
(*Stadtbildstelle, Essen*)

Opposite: Interior of the Essen Synagogue.
(*Courtesy of Dr Edina Meyer, Tel Aviv*)

Right: New Consistorial Synagogue, Paris. In 1852 this structure replaced the old synagogue of rue Notre Dame de Nazareth which had fallen into disrepair. It had two tiers of galleries, the lower one for a surplus of men worshippers and the upper one for women. It was influenced by both Romanesque and Oriental styles.
(*Illustrierte Zeitung, Leipzig, May 1852*)

Above: Exterior of the Beth Elohim Synagogue, Charleston, South Carolina. This handsome building, built in 1840, was inspired by Greek temple architecture. (*American Jewish Archives, Cincinnati*)

Below: Plum Street Temple of Congregation B'nai Jeshurun, Cincinnati, built in 1848. This is one of the outstanding examples of Moorish synagogue architecture in the United States. (*American Jewish Archives, Cincinnati*)

Above: First Ashkenazi Synagogue in New York, B'nai Jeshurun, on Elm Street near Canal Street, consecrated in 1827 by a group that seceded from the Sephardi Shearith Israel Congregation. The building had belonged to the African Church, a Protestant Mission for blacks. (*Museum of the City of New York*)

Opposite: The façade of Temple Emanu-El, New York, combining Gothic, Romanesque and Byzantine styles. The large windows in its western wall have become a Fifth Avenue landmark. (*Beth Hatefutsoth Archive, Tel Aviv/Photo: Theodore Cohen*)

longer central and even religious education began to be organized by the community rather than the synagogue.

The first Ashkenazi synagogues were converted church buildings such as New York's B'nai Jeshurun which acquired the 'African Church' on Elm Street in 1826. From the 1830s Reform Judaism was introduced by Jews of German origin who were now the dominant element. This followed the pattern set in Europe: women sat with men, organs and mixed choirs were introduced, second days of holidays, fasting, and the wearing of the *tefillin* (phylacteries) were abolished; the sermons and much of the liturgy were in English, prayers for the Messiah and the Return to Zion were omitted, Torah readings were shortened, and services were often held on Sundays instead of Saturdays. The large central platform disappeared (except among the Sephardim and the extreme Orthodox who were, however, a

negligible element until the 1880s). The buildings resembled their European counterparts with the reader's desk combined with the ark platform, family pews across the hall, and organ and choir loft above the ark.

The styles of architecture also generally corresponded to those currently popular in Europe. One contrast was the greater use of the neo-Gothic style which in the absence of old churches was not so redolent of Christianity in the United States. Notable examples included Cincinnati's B'nai Jeshurun built in 1848 and New York's twin-towered Anshe Chesed Synagogue, opened in Norfolk Street in 1850. The neo-Classical style evoked buildings inspired by both Roman and Greek examples. From the outside, some of the synagogues, such as Beth Elohim in Charleston (1840) and the Baltimore Hebrew Congregation (1845) with its Doric porticoes, recalled majestic Greek temples.

European Jews also brought oriental fashions to American synagogues. At first the Egyptian style was favoured, ranging from Philadelphia's 1825 Mikveh Israel, with columns copied from an Egyptian temple, to the same city's Beth Israel, built in 1849. The Byzantine trend was set by the bulbous domes of Philadelphia's Knesseth Israel (1864) and San Francisco's Temple Emanu-El (1866, destroyed in the 1906 earthquake). The first Moorish synagogue was Cincinnati's Plum Street Temple, described as 'an Alhambra temple with slender pillars and thirteen domes corresponding to the thirteen attributes of God'. In his dedication sermon the father of Reform Judaism in the United States, Isaac M. Wise, explained the difference between a synagogue and a temple: 'Worship in a temple is conducted in gladness, not in perpetual mourning as in the synagogue.' Another object of the temple, he explained, was to proclaim the universal religion of the future, which would be patterned after the faith of Israel. The biggest controversy in the new building concerned the covering of heads; by majority vote it was decided to pray bare-headed, but three of the oldest congregants were allowed to wear hats

to the end of their days. The 1868 building of New York's Temple Emanu-El (at Fifth Avenue and 43rd Street) was inspired by the Alhambra with its horseshoe arches and deep-blue ceiling. A feature that evoked wonder and pride was the lighting which resulted from the burning of five hundred gas jets. Another New York synagogue in the Islamic tradition, the Central Synagogue, remains a landmark on Lexington Avenue and 55th Street.

From the 1880s the East Europeans brought their *shtiebls*, the unpretentious prayer rooms. The *shul* was the centre of life for many of them, and even when situated in the top storey of some decrepit tenement slum still sought to provide a whole range of services for its members. The more ambitious took over synagogues no longer used by German Jews who had moved away to more prosperous neighbourhoods. The new edifices built by the 'old-timers' often discarded the mélange of styles that had characterized the nineteenth-century synagogue and tended to the classical. Jewish architects now came to the fore and some of them designed striking synagogues. They included Arnold Brunner (whose distinguished Shearith Israel Synagogue, built in 1897, still stands on Central Park West in New York), Dankmar Adler (who with Louis Sullivan pioneered a simplified synagogue design in 1890-1 for Anshe Maariv Congregation in Chicago), and Albert Kahn (who designed the Detroit Beth-El Synagogue in 1922).

The 1920s saw some magnificent structures across the country, from the cathedral-like (100 ft × 200 ft) basilica of Temple Emanu-El in New York (built in 1929 on Fifth Avenue and 65th Street) to San Francisco's Temple Emanu-El (1926) which introduced Californian elements into the more familiar exotic style. In general, however, synagogue architecture in the United States was not innovative between the two Wars. The atmosphere of the Depression and the situation in Europe were not conducive to experimentation or investment in large buildings. The next major developments came only after the Second World War.

~ II ~

MEETING MODERN CHALLENGES

THE Nazis were dedicated not only to exterminating the Jewish people but also to destroying expressions of their culture, and at the top of their list stood the synagogues. They did not wait for the excuse of war to embark on their programme but by November 1938 were prepared to use the murder of a German diplomat in Paris as a pretext to order élite troops to burn down the synagogues in Germany, Austria, and Sudetenland, those parts of Europe then under their control. This night of horror became known as *Kristallnacht*, or the night of the broken glass, because of the damage wrought on Jewish property in the rampage.

Attacks on synagogues had occurred even earlier that year. On 9 June the Great Synagogue of Munich was destroyed on Hitler's personal orders, and this was followed by the demolition of synagogues in Nuremberg and Dortmund. But on 9 November orders went out to burn down all synagogues, and the sole proviso that accompanied them was that German life and property was to be spared. Fire brigades were ordered to stand by, with instructions to stop flames spreading to 'Aryan' property, but in no way to hinder the blaze in the synagogues.

In the previous chapter the Kaiser's interest in the construction of the synagogue at Potsdam was mentioned. Now, years later, an official of that same synagogue was taken by the Gestapo to the building at 5.30 a.m. He subsequently described his experience as follows:

A dark group of Catiline-like figures in mufti was already assembled there. They all carried mysterious-looking instruments. The main synagogue door had resisted the attack of between twenty and twenty-five men so that I was forced to show the leaders a side entrance. They smashed the door down and I led the ringleader through the back entrance into the synagogue. Evidently it was not impressive enough for the leader of the mob. He shouted to me 'We want to see the Holy of Holies'. By now the mob at the front entrance had pushed its way in. A fearful scene was played out with uncanny speed. In a few minutes the entire interior was transformed into a heap of ruins. All the windows were smashed, the chandeliers pulled from the ceiling, the benches chopped up, the women's gallery demolished, the rabbi's seat hacked to pieces, the curtains torn down, the scrolls of the Law ripped into shreds, the great candelabrum used as a battering ram. Nothing was left unharmed. It was so terrible and bestial that the leader of the group – who could not be considered soft-hearted – said 'We'd better go'. As we left, small tongues of flames were licking their way upward in the foyer.[1]

This terrible scene was repeated hundreds of times. The Nazi leader, Heydrich, who had directed the operation, reported to his superiors that 76 synagogues had been destroyed completely and 191 set on fire, but the number was probably greater. The great monuments of

1. Lionel Kochan, *Progrom: November 10, 1938*, André Deutsch, London 1957.

Above left: The ruins of Hanover synagogue, one of the most majestic in Germany, built in 1870 and enlarged in 1900, after Crystal Night.
(*Historisches Museum, Hanover*)

Above right: The Great Synagogue in Danzig marked for destruction by the Nazis. Inaugurated in 1887, it was dismantled after the tragic end of the community in 1939. The signs read: 'The synagogue will be torn down' and 'Come dear Mary and free us of the Jews'. (The Jews were ordered to leave the city by May 1939.)
(*Jewish Museum, New York*)

Left: Crystal Night, 9/10 November 1938. In one night hundreds of synagogues in Germany and Austria were burned down by the Nazis. This photograph shows the destruction of the synagogue in Siegen, Germany.
(*Archive, Kibbutz Lohamei Hagettaot*)

Opposite: Interior of the Belfast Synagogue, built in 1964.
(*Courtesy of Keter Publishing House*)

German Jewry, built with so much care, thought and love, lay in ruins.

This, however, was only the beginning. Less than a year later the war started and wherever German forces entered, one of their first targets was the Jewish place of worship. Synagogues were systematically destroyed – sometimes with their congregations inside – not only by the SS Storm Troopers but by regular troops, and not only by Germans but by their collaborators in other countries. In some places 'fire brigades' were formed – not to put out fires but to start them. The destruction was accompanied by vandalism and looting; not only were the buildings destroyed but their often precious contents, including priceless ritual objects, disappeared forever. Some synagogues were saved because they were converted for other uses – pleasure-houses for the soldiers or stables for the horses.

No synagogues were permitted in the ghettos into which the Jews were herded, and collective worship was forbidden. But the Jews never ceased their prayers and, at danger to their lives, they gathered in clandestine *minyanim* (prayer quorums), even in the ghettos, the deportation centres, the forced labour and death camps. This was true especially on the High Holidays when they found ways to come together and pray under the very noses of the Germans.

There was further damage to synagogues in other parts of Europe, from air and land bombardments, augmenting the tragedy of the annihilation of the synagogues of Europe. Noted eighteenth-century synagogues in London, Leghorn, and Rotterdam came to an untimely end in this way.

After the war was over, the Jewish world found itself in completely new circumstances. The great European centre had been largely wiped out. Occasionally a synagogue building had survived, only to be without a community or with too small and impoverished a congregation to be able to maintain it. In one or two instances, these buildings were turned into museums but more usually they were adapted

for some other purpose or razed to the ground. Throughout Eastern Europe, wrecked or decaying buildings can still be found – the remains of pre-war synagogues.

The Jewish population all over the world was on the move after the war and new centres sprang up where Jews had never lived before, for a variety of reasons. In London, for example, the Blitz delivered the death blow to the already diminished Jewish population in the East End, once the effervescent centre of Anglo-Jewry. Today the Jews praying in the historic Bevis Marks Synagogue arrive from distant parts of the city. It is in the suburbs and the new satellite towns of Great Britain that Jews largely live now and build their synagogues. The new synagogues servicing West Germany's thirty thousand Jews are mostly small (especially when compared with their predecessors) and often include the community centre and social facilities. Sometimes they stand on the site of the old synagogue and

incorporate pitiful remains. The ancient synagogue at Worms has been painstakingly reconstructed, but as a site to be visited, not as a
place of prayer. A quorum of Jews cannot be
raised in the city.

The notable exception to the general picture
of stagnation and retreat on the Continent has
been in France, where the community has been
galvanized by the arrival of hundreds of
thousands of Jews who abandoned the less
hospitable climes of North Africa. The majority of the country's half-million Jews are
Sephardim, who have established communities
in many new centres and revived others which
had been dormant for centuries, especially in
southern France. In some places disused synagogues have been brought back to life, while
elsewhere new ones have been founded, carrying on the styles and tradition familiar in North
Africa.

In one alarming respect a retrogression has
occurred, and synagogues have again become a
frequent object of hostile attack. The culprits
are not the mobs of former times but hit-
and-run terrorists who have singled out the
synagogues in Europe as a target for their
anti-Jewish and anti-Zionist campaigns. Loss
of life, serious injury, and widespread damage
have been inflicted on synagogues and worshippers in Western and Central Europe,
Scandinavia, and Italy. It is now usual for
synagogues to be under constant police guard,
with strict security precautions applied at the
entrance. In some cases their external appearance is marred by protective walls and fences.

In Eastern Europe there are great differences
between the fate of synagogues and synagogue
life in the socialist republics and in the Soviet
Union. In the former, the Jewish community
has been legitimized and the government sub-
sidizes the religious needs of its Jews, including
care for their houses of worship. Numbers may
have dwindled and religious functionaries may
be in short supply but synagogues are kept up
and some of the magnificent buildings which
have survived in Budapest, Szeged, Bucharest,
Sofia, and East Berlin, for example, are in

regular use. Prague's Altneuschul is the oldest synagogue where services are held; the other venerable Prague synagogues now house the Czech State Jewish Museum.

In Russia the story is very different. As far back as 1918 the houses of worship of all faiths were entrusted to the local Soviets to decide their use. A bitter internal struggle ensued between religious Jews and communist Jews (the 'Yevsektzia'), with the latter conducting anti-synagogue propaganda as part of their general anti-religious campaign. Sometimes this even resulted in fist-fights as the Yevsektzia Jews tried to prevent worshippers from entering their places of worship or praying there. The Soviet government imposed severe restrictions, dissolving Jewish communities and rescinding all national and religious privileges

Opposite: The bombed entrance to the Copenhagen Synagogue after a terrorist attack, 1985. (*Photo: André Brutmann*)

Below: Interior view of the synagogue at Tashkent, Uzbekistan, U.S.S.R., 1983. (*Beth Hatefutsoth Archive, Tel Aviv/Photo: Theodore Cohen*)

that had been granted in the pre-Soviet period. Synagogues that remained open were subject to harassment and offensive demonstrations were held outside while prayers were in progress. Ritual objects were confiscated and prayer books became a rarity; to reprint them was forbidden. The conversion of synagogues into buildings for secular purpose was undertaken on a large scale from the late 1920s and hundreds were converted within a few years. The Soviets contended that they were 'yielding to popular demand', as communist Jews demonstrated, demanding the closure of synagogues portrayed as 'clubs of profiteers'. Those that remained open were administered by a committee responsible to the local authorities. Activities were severely limited and worshippers became legally vulnerable in view of the ban on 'religious propaganda' or on religious education for children.

The exception to all this hostility was in Asiatic Russia. The Jews tucked away in Georgia, Uzbekistan, and other remote regions, far away from both the Jewish and Soviet nerve centres, were, like practitioners of other religions, allowed to continue their traditional way of life. Their synagogues were small prayer houses often colourfully decorated with carpets and rugs, resembling those elsewhere in the Middle East such as Kurdistan, Iraq, and Iran. They served as 'places of assembly' for the entire community, from the elders to the children. During the Second World War many Jews were evacuated to this region from the areas occupied by the Germans, both in the Soviet Union proper and in the countries it had occupied during the first years of the war, including eastern Poland and the Baltic states. As the prayer rites of the newcomers were different, they organized their own places of worship. Formally these new places of worship were not legal, but they were tolerated during the Second World War and, once established, were allowed to continue.

The anti-Jewish policies promulgated during Stalin's last years and during the time of his successors led to the closing of most of the four hundred synagogues which remained in Soviet Russia at the end of the war. Only about sixty were permitted to remain open, more than forty of them in Georgia, the Caucasus, and Central Asia. Cities with large Jewish populations were allowed no more than a single synagogue. As in the pre-war period, the authorities claimed that they were acting in accordance with the wishes of the community and accused the synagogues of being 'nests of corruption', now further alleging that they were 'centres of pro-Israel propaganda'.

It was Israel that gave Soviet Jewish identity its greatest fillip and this was expressed most openly from the late 1960s precisely at the remaining synagogues. Despite the long campaign of hate and threats, of indoctrination and brainwashing, the Jewish youth in the Soviet Union insisted on an open expression of their Jewishness and their identification with the State of Israel, and they chose to express this both inside and outside the synagogues, especially on the festival of Simhat Torah (the

Park Synagogue, Cleveland, Ohio, designed by Erich Mendelsohn in 1948. This was planned as a hemispheric dome enclosing the synagogue proper and rising from a long, low, flat-roofed structure.
(*Beth Hatefutsoth Archive, Tel Aviv*)

Rejoicing of the Law). The main focus was in Moscow where tens of thousands of young Jews flocked to the streets around the synagogue to dance and sing Hebrew and Yiddish songs. The Soviet police at first tried harassment, but when this proved to be of no avail, they accepted the situation and contented themselves with cordoning off the area. The scene was repeated in other large towns. Never in its long history had the synagogues been the centre of such expression of defiance, pride, determination, and hope.

In the United States of America where almost half the world's Jews live, the synagogue experienced a revival following the Second World War. This was due not so much to religious effervescence as to social circumstances; it was an emulation of the 'back to church' movement among the Christians. Going to a place of worship was 'in' and the Jews joined the trend. The synagogue, for its part, adapted itself to this new situation by reverting to its multifunctional role as in pre-Emancipation days. The American Jewish thinker, Mordecai M. Kaplan, propounded the concept of the 'synagogue centre', insisting that in the modern world the synagogue had to be more than a house of prayer. It had once again to be a 'house of assembly' in a contemporary reformulation, a centre of Jewish social, cultural, and recreational life. The members of the community would spend much of their leisure time within its walls. The prayer hall (and often another small chapel for weekday services) was the seat of only one branch of bustling activity. Synagogue buildings now had social halls, classrooms, gymnasia and swimming pools (a temple in Oklahoma City is popularly called 'the *shul* with a pool'), bookshops and libraries, museums and art galleries. The staff includes not only the rabbi and cantor but educational, social and administrative personnel. As in former times, the synagogue resembles a beehive, events going on throughout the day and evening.

Innovative programming demanded and

received innovative design. As the Jews moved out to the suburbs, they needed their centres in the new places of residence. This suited the planners who required greater space than was available in the inner city. The new synagogues with their attendant facilities were laid out over a considerable area, often surrounded by ample lawns (not to mention car-parks, used on the Sabbath as well as on weekdays). The impact was one of spaciousness and airiness. Entrance was not from the street but through the grounds of the complex. The often horizontally-shaped buildings replaced the fussiness or monumentality of their predecessors with smooth, straight lines. Simplicity was preferred to ornateness. One innovation was the collapsible wall of the sanctuary (as the prayer hall was now often called). When, as on the High Holidays, there was a large attendance, one wall – usually the western wall – could be removed, thus incorporating the adjacent social hall into the synagogue. Inside the synagogue or temple greater unity was obtained by dispensing with the women's gallery. Even in Orthodox synagogues, the tendency was to separate the women on the main floor, at the sides or at the back, but not to construct special galleries for them. Sometimes the entire complex would be constructed around an interior court.

Noted architects have been influential in determining the direction of synagogue design. An important pioneer was Erich Mendelsohn who, after working in Germany and Palestine, moved to the United States after the Second World War. His B'nai Amoonah Synagogue in St Louis with its soaring parabolic roof, the Park Synagogue, Cleveland, and a number of Jewish centres brought the functional design of Europe to the modern synagogue. Louis I. Kahn designed an austere fortress-like building for Congregation Mikveh Israel, in Philadelphia. Outstanding non-Jewish architects also turned their attention to the synagogue, among them Frank Lloyd Wright, whose building for Beth Shalom, Elkins Park, Pennsylvania, is

The interior of Beth Shalom Congregation Synagogue, Elkins Park, illustrating how exterior motifs, like the use of triangular shapes, are continued in the interior. (*Keter Publishing House, Jerusalem*)

Above: Beth Shalom Congregation Synagogue, Elkins Park, Pennsylvania, built in 1959 to the design of Frank Lloyd Wright.
(*Beth Hatefutsoth model/Photo: Michael Horton*)

Opposite: The ark in the International Synagogue at Kennedy Airport, New York, 1963. This is one of a cluster of three religious buildings, including a Catholic and a Protestant chapel. There is a similar group at Brandeis University, Waltham, Massachusetts.
(*Beth Hatefutsoth Archive, Tel Aviv/Photo: Theodore Cohen*)

Above: Façade of the Baltimore Hebrew Congregation. The eight panels sculpted by George Aarons symbolize the ethical message of Judaism. In the centre, the first five commandments of the Decalogue concerning man's relationship with God, are represented by flames, and the last five, concerning man's relationship with man, by earth. The lower panel represents the creation of man. Other subjects are: (*left, top to bottom*) loyalty (Ruth and Naomi), the Law, Exodus; (*right*) justice (Nathan and David), peace (swords into ploughshares) and obedience (Abraham and Isaac).
(*Keter Publishing House, Jerusalem*)

Opposite: Mount Sinai Temple, El Paso, Texas. Built in 1962 to the design of Sidney Eisenstat, it is prominent against its desert background.
(*Courtesy of Sidney Eisenstat, Beverly Hills, California*)

Below left: Interior of Congregation Israel, North Shore, Glencoe, Illinois, designed by Japanese-American architect Minoru Yamasaki and built in 1964. Attention is focused on the gilded teak ark whose pen-like shape may be symbolic of the art of the Torah scribe.
(*Union of American Hebrew Congregations, New York*)

Below right: Women rabbi: Rabbi Kinneret Shiryon officiating at a Reform service in Ramat Aviv, Israel, 1986.
(*Photo: Lisa Pleskow*)

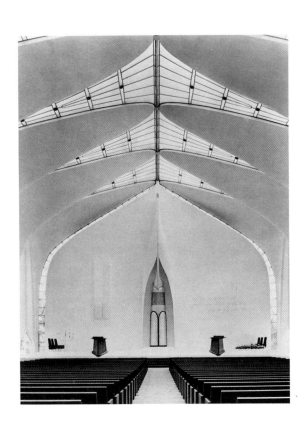

topped with a glass-sheathed tower inspired by Mount Sinai and by the concept of the Tent of Meeting. The most popular designer has been Percival Goodman, whose many synagogues tend to be small and friendly, radiating a warm atmosphere.

In its aesthetic quest one of the most striking developments of the American synagogue has been the artist's participation in ornamentation. The graphic and plastic arts have come into their own. These are exemplified in sculptures, especially at the approach to the buildings or on their exterior walls, and in the ritual objects: the covers for the ark and the Torah scroll, the eternal light before the ark, and the candelabra. Many of America's greatest artists – Jews and non-Jews – have contributed to this artistic efflorescence which enhances the religious experience by combining beauty with holiness. Traditional Jewish themes are reflected in the paintings, sculptures, mosaics, tapestries, and stained glass windows. A new feature in many synagogues is a Holocaust memorial, often in the form of a six-branched candelabrum symbolizing the six million victims.

In recent years a need has been felt, especially among the younger generation, for more intimate surroundings than can be found in the usual synagogue. In the framework of liturgical and social experimentation, they are praying in small *minyanim*. An example of this development can be found in New York's Anshe Chesed Synagogue where a large, venerable building has been split up into three small synagogues, each congregation seeking its own emphasis and expression. Another significant change in the American synagogue has been the emergence of women as religious functionaries. In the Conservative, Reconstructionist, and Reform congregations, which account for the large majority of American synagogues and temples, women rabbis and women cantors officiate. Women are counted as members of a *minyan*, and are called up to the reading of the Law as part of the increasingly egalitarian scene.

In modern Israel, too, the synagogue has had to adapt itself to new roles. Throughout the Diaspora it served as the central expression of Jewish identity and since the Emancipation many joined synagogues not as a religious expression but as a proclamation of their Jewishness. For Jews in Israel such a declaration is not necessary – the very act of living in Israel is a statement of one's Jewishness. Moreover, the various services traditionally provided by the synagogue, apart from the act of worship, are now automatically received: the State is responsible for Jewish education and law courts, religious or otherwise; the rabbinate deals with *kashrut*; the local authorities with burial; the sick funds with hospitalization; and social life is cared for by various factors. The synagogue is, therefore, almost exclusively a place of prayer for those who choose to congregate within its walls. It is paradoxical that precisely in the Jewish state the synagogue has lost the central position it held during the centuries in the Diaspora. Its restriction to the function of prayer means that fewer demands are made on the architect and planner. Already at the end of the nineteenth century the small synagogues that sprung up in the new Jewish neighbourhoods of Jerusalem, each serving a well-defined community, lacked originality. In the *moshavot*, the early agricultural settlements, a synagogue would be built in the main street but it was a simple building reflecting the Spartan lifestyle of the pioneers.

Under British rule (1917–48) the new towns and the religious settlements were the main initiators of synagogues, and by 1948 the country had eight hundred Jewish places of worship. These tended to be undistinguished until the 1930s when Palestinian architecture began to be influenced by Modernism and synagogues started to reflect new styles, techniques, and materials. The first outstanding examples were the Great Synagogue in Tel Aviv (c.1930) and the Yeshurun Synagogue in Jerusalem (1934), whose modern design was in striking contrast to the previous lack of originality.

Following the establishment of the state in 1948, the arrival of Jews from many parts of the world posed new challenges. At first, the immigrants' transit camps had to be supplied with appropriate facilities, usually of a makeshift nature, and services were often held in tin huts or tents. After moving to permanent quarters, each community expected to reproduce the synagogue it had left behind, both in its general appearance and in its mode of service. In all aspects of life the authorities were

Opposite, far left: Great Synagogue, Tel Aviv, built in *c.*1930, whose modernist and monumental style was a turning point in synagogue design in Palestine. (*Central Zionist Archive, Jerusalem*)

Opposite: Yeshurun Synagogue in Jerusalem, 1934, whose modern design was an innovation in synagogue building in that city. Its windows were kept small both for security and because of the strong sunlight. (*Courtesy of Yeshurun Synagogue, Jerusalem*)

Above: Synagogue at an Israel army officer training school, Mitzpeh Ramon, designed by the architect Zvi Hecker in 1969. A small synagogue, holding 120 worshippers, its exterior is structured like a crystal and is coloured green, yellow and grey, contrasting with the monotonous desert landscape that surrounds it. (*Courtesy of Zvi Hecker, Tel Aviv*)

wrestling with the problem of whether to encourage a 'melting pot' approach, aiming at synthesis, or to leave the different communities to foster the traditions they had brought with them. In synagogue life the communities answered this for themselves by establishing their own places of worship. In some places Jewish labourers, after finishing their day's work, got together to build their own synagogue. In centres of mixed population efforts were made to cater to all the groups, even if each had only a modest room. Sometimes, as in Ashkelon, a single building incorporated several synagogues, each catering to a different tradition.

In the Israeli army it was felt that chaos and dislocation would result if each recruit were to be provided with praying facilities according to his ethnic background. Moreover, this flew in the face of the army's objective of unifying soldiers from disparate backgrounds. The solution was the creation of a unified prayer

Opposite, above: Israel Goldstein Synagogue on the Givat Ram campus of the Hebrew University designed by Heinz Rau. The windowless synagogue, whose light comes from below, is in the upper part of the building. (*Hebrew University, Jerusalem/Photo: Werner Braun*)

Opposite, below: The synagogue in Beersheba, built in 1961 and used by a mixed Ashkenazi-Sephardi congregation. (*Photo: Amiram Harlap*)

Right: The Ohel Aharon Synagogue in the Israel Institute of Technology, built in 1969. (*Photo: Amiram Harlap*)

Below: Hechal Yehuda Synagogue in Tel Aviv, built in 1980, whose shell-shape reflects its seaside location. Its congregation originated in Salonica, Greece. (*Photo: Amiram Harlap*)

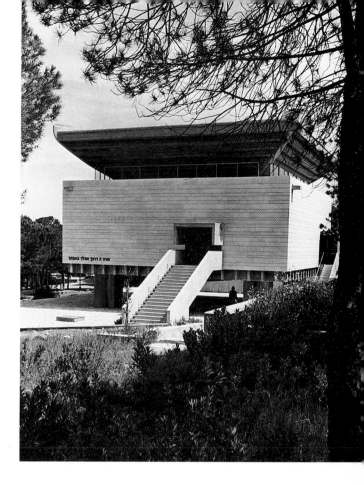

rite, designed to satisfy all communities, and the erection of a single military synagogue in every camp. Much thought was given to its form and the traditional Jewish symbols were combined with those of the State and the Israel Defence Forces. A portable synagogue was developed for use under field and battle conditions.

The rapid growth of Israel's variegated population necessitated the opening of a vast number of synagogues, of which Jerusalem retained the greatest concentration. In the 1950s there was a professor from the Hebrew University who made it a point to pray in a different synagogue every day – and it took him well over a year to complete the circuit. More recently, as communal differences become less pronounced, and a new generation with a shared past reaches maturity, one large synagogue may cater for an entire community.

Israel's major new synagogues have been influenced by styles prevailing in the West. Since modern architecture is international in character, it is natural that the inspiration for many of Israel's synagogues can be found elsewhere. Sometimes the architect has drawn his model from the past: the domes and forecourts recall synagogues of old. Some of the buildings evoke fortress synagogues; the Belz synagogue under construction in Jerusalem is directly modelled on the original building in Belz; and the four Ben-Zakkai synagogues in the Old City of Jerusalem (see Chapter VIII) are not precise reconstructions but modern halls evoking the atmosphere of the originals.

To make the buildings distinctive, familiar symbols – the tablets of the Law, the Star of David, and especially the candelabrum, now the symbol of the State of Israel – are prominently displayed on the exterior. Internally the patterns are familiar: the ark along the wall facing the Temple Mount, the reader's desk in the centre of the rectangular hall, the women in a back or side gallery or partitioned off at ground level. In sharp contrast to the United States, there is no creative partnership between

the synagogue and the sculptor and artist, and when the Israeli synagogue has original artistic expression, it is the exception. Occasionally stained glass windows are to be found, most notably in Jerusalem's Hadassah Synagogue where Marc Chagall's twelve windows on the theme of the Twelve Tribes is a work of art of

Interior of the Great Synagogue, Jerusalem, dedicated in
1982.
(*Courtesy of the Great Synagogue, Jerusalem*)

international renown. Many Orthodox authorities, however, continue to frown on such
'distractions' from the main foci, that is, the
platform and the ark, and it is these which have
attracted the main artistic attention especially
through decorations for the ark (such as the
curtain and scroll covers). Some synagogues

incorporate furnishings rescued from European synagogues, including twenty-eight arks from Italy.

As we conclude this survey of the world of the synagogue, extending over more than two millennia, we find the institution still vital and vibrant, and playing a central role in Jewish life, although not the monolithic role it played, for the most part, in the pre-Emancipation era. In the modern world it has developed in three different directions. In North America it has regained its traditional community functions which for a time it had surrendered to other aegises. In Israel it has lost its communal functions, now taken over largely by the authorities, and has become essentially a place of prayer. In the U.S.S.R., where generations have been raised in an atmosphere hostile to religion, the surviving synagogues have retained for the younger generations a significance as the only visible symbol through which they can express their ethnic identification. Each of the three centres personifies in its own way the integral role of the synagogue in the long history of Jewish continuity.

A class in the Hecht Synagogue on the Hebrew University's Mount Scopus campus. The two arks are on either side of a picture window over looking the Temple Mount.
(*Hebrew University, Jerusalem/Photo: David Harris*)

GLOSSARY

ARK: Place in the Synagogue where the Scrolls of the Law are kept, usually covered by a curtain.

ASHKENAZIM (adjective, Ashkenazi): Jews originating from medieval Germany and its environs; the synagogue rite of these Jews (as distinct from Sephardi, q.v.)

BATLANIM (literally 'men of leisure'): Originally, men who could devote themselves to community and synagogue affairs. In time, applied to poor or unemployed Jews who were paid to attend synagogue and ensure a prayer quorum.

BENE ISRAEL ('Sons of Israel'): Indian Jewish community originating along the Konkan coast, south of Bombay.

BIMA: Reader's platform in the synagogue.

CABBALA: Jewish mysticism. A proponent of Cabbala is known as a cabbalist.

DAY OF ATONEMENT (in Hebrew, Yom Kippur): Most solemn day in the Jewish calendar, observed by a twenty-four-hour fast. The day is spent in the synagogue as, according to Jewish belief, on this day God records the fate of every individual for the coming year.

DIASPORA: The Jewish people living outside the Land of Israel.

ETROG: The citron fruit; one of the Four Species (q.v.).

FOUR SPECIES: The citron fruit and branches of the palm, willow and myrtle trees carried in procession on the Tabernacles holiday.

GE'EZ (Old Ethiopic): Language of the sacred books of the Jews of Ethiopia.

GENIZA: Place for storing worn-out scrolls and religious books.

HAFTARA: Selection from the Prophetical Books of the Bible, read in the synagogue in the Sabbath service.

HANUKKA: Festival celebrating the victory of the Maccabees.

HASIDISM: Pietist movement originating in Eastern Europe in the eighteenth century. Its adherents were called Hasidim.

HOSHANA RABBA: Seventh day of the Feast of Tabernacles, an occasion for processions around the synagogue.

KABBALA see Cabbala.

KARAITES: Jewish sect originating in the eighth century which maintained the literal meaning of the Bible and rejected rabbinical interpretations.

KASHRUT: Jewish dietary laws.

LAG BA-OMER: The thirty-third day of the Omer, the period of semi-mourning between Passover and Pentecost (Shavuot). This is a minor festival on which mourning customs are suspended and weddings are permitted.

MAGEN DAVID ('Star of David'): The Hexagram; a mystical symbol from ancient times, it became a major Jewish symbol in recent centuries.

MARRANOS: Name given to Jews in Spain and Portugal who were forced to adopt Christianity in the fifteenth century but continued to practice Judaism in secret.

MATZA (plural *matzot*): Unleavened bread, eaten during the Passover festival.

MENORA: A candelabrum. In the Temple, the seven-branched candelabrum was one of the main ritual objects and in ancient times was the leading Jewish symbol. Later, an eight-branched candelabrum was used for the Hanukka festival.

MISHNA: Codification of the Oral Law, dating from c.200 AD.

MINYAN: The Jewish prayer quorum of ten adult males (modern Reform and some Conservative congregations count females in the quorum).

ORAL LAW: Legal and other traditions believed by Jews to have been given by God to Moses on Mount Sinai, coexistent with the Written Law contained in the Pentateuch.

PENTATEUCH: The five books of Moses, the first part of the Hebrew Bible.

PURIM: Spring festival commemorating the salvation of the Jews of the Persian Empire, as related in the Book of Esther.

RABBANITES: The rabbinical opponents of the Karaites (q.v.).

REBBE: Yiddish form of 'rabbi', used by Hasidim.

SCROLL OF THE LAW (in Hebrew, *Sefer Torah*): Handwritten scroll of the Pentateuch used for public reading in the synagogue; when not in use, kept in the ark.

SEPHARDIM (adjective Sephardi): Jews originating from Spain and Portugal, the synagogue rites of these Jews (as distinct from Ashkenazi, q.v.).

SHAVUOT: Feast of Weeks of Pentecost. A summer harvest festival, also commemorating the Giving of the Law on Mount Sinai.

SHEMA ('Hear'): Judaism's basic statement of faith proclaiming the unity of God (Deuteronomy 6:4).

SHOFAR: Ram's horn, sounded in the synagogue on the New Year and other solemn occasions.

SHTETL: Small town or village in eastern Europe with a largely Jewish population.

SHTIEBL (Yiddish 'small room'): The small one-room synagogue of the Hasidim.

SHUL: Yiddish word for synagogue.

SIMHAT TORAH ('Rejoicing of the Law'): Feast day when the annual cycle of the Pentateuch reading in the synagogue is concluded and a new cycle begun.

TABLETS OF THE LAW: Stone tablets given by God to Moses on Mount Sinai on which were inscribed the Ten Commandments. In recent centuries, an artistic representation was frequently featured in the synagogue.

TALMUD: The major corpus of Jewish religious law, second in authority only to the Bible.

TEMPLE: First Temple, built by King Solomon as the focus of the Israelite worship; destroyed by the Babylonians under Nebuchadnezzar in 586 BC; Second Temple built 539–515 BC; major reconstruction by Herod, 1st century BC; destroyed by Romans under Titus in AD 70.

TEN DAYS OF PENITENCE: Period from the New Year to the Day of Atonement, a period for repentance.

TWELVE TRIBES: Early division of the Israelites according to their descent from the sons of Jacob.

YEVSEKTZIA: Jewish section of the propaganda department of the Russian communist party, 1918–30.

ZIONISM: Movement aiming at the return of the Jewish People to the Land of Israel.

INDEX

Numbers in *italics* refer to
illustrations and captions

Abulafia, Samuel Halevi, 66
Aden Synagogue, *144*
Adler, Dankmar, 184
Aleppo, Great Synagogue, *137*, *141*,
  142–3
Alexandria, 10, *142*; Great
  Synagogue, *10*; Prophet Elijah
  Synagogue, *140*, *142*
Alfonso X of Castile, 58
Algiers synagogues, 135, 176
Alibag, Magen Aboth Synagogue,
  151, *151–2*, 153
Altdorfer, Albrecht, 46
Altneuschul, Prague, 46, *46–9*, 50,
  94, *177*, 189
Amsterdam, *114–22*; Ashkenazi
  Great Synagogue, 120, *120–1*;
  Ets Haim Library, 120;
  Portuguese Synagogue ('Talmud
  Torah'), 114, *116*, 117;
  Portuguese Synagogue
  ('Esnoga'), 117, *118–19*, 120,
  120–1, 122, 124
Ancona synagogues, 74, 75, 79, 80
Ansbach communal synagogue, 168
Ark, sacred, 20, 22, 24, 34, 36, 38,
  39, 40, 46, 52, 53, 59, *59*, 62, 63,
  66, 73, 75, 80, 81, *84–92*, 96, 97,
  99, 104, *113*, *123*, 132, *137*, *142*,
  144, 146, 155, *159*, 163, 170, 181,
  193, *194*, 195, 200, *201–2*, *202*;
  multiple/double, 132, *136*
Art Nouveau synagogue, Paris, 180
Ashkelon synagogues, 198
Ashkenaz, 37–55, 58, 74

Babylonian exile, 9, 10, 17
Babylonian synagogues, 27, 35, 37
Baghdad, 131, 143; Great
  Synagogue, 133, *142*, 143
Baltimore Hebrew Congregation,
  182, *194*
Baram Synagogue, *18–19*, *18–19*, 25
Basevi, George, 180
batlanim (paid member of
  congregation), 50
Beersheba Synagogue, *198*
Belfast Synagogue, *187*
Belisario, I.M., *123*
Belmonte synagogue, 71

Belz fortress synagogue, Poland,
  104–5, 200
Belz Synagogue, Jerusalem, 200
Ben Asher, Jacob, 75
Ben Asher codex, *142–3*
Ben Ezra Synagogue (Maimonides
  Synagogue), Cairo, 138, *139*, 140
Bene Israel Jews, 149–53
Benjamin of Tudela, 138, 143, 144
Ben-Zakkai, *see* Johanan Ben-
  Zakkai
Berlin, 188; Fasanenstrasse
  Temple, *178*; Heidereutergasse
  Synagogue, 168, *168*;
  Oranienburgerstrasse
  Synagogue, 166, 176
Bet Alfa mosaics, 21, 24, 25, 29
Beta Israel Jews (Falashas), 163–5
beth midrash of Israel Baal Shem
  Tov, *110*
'Birds' Head Haggada', Germany,
  38
blessing the moon ceremony, 53, *55*
Boener, Johann Alexander, *51*
Bohemian synagogues, 37, 46–50,
  110
Bombay, *148*, 149–51, 153;
  Knesseth Elijah Synagogue, *148*;
  Magen David Synagogue, *152*;
  Magen Hasidim Synagogue, *150*,
  151; New Synagogue, *149*; Rodef
  Shalom Synagogue, 151; Shaar
  Harahamim Synagogue, 149;
  Tifereth Israel Synagogue, 149,
  150
Brody fortress synagogue, *105*
Brunner, Arnold, 184
Budapest, 188; Alt-Ofen
  Synagogue, *172*; Dohany Street
  Synagogue, *171*, *174*; Synagogue
  in Obuda, *173*
Byzantine period/style, 19, 21, 174,
  183, 184

Cagliari synagogue, 73
Cairo, 131, 138–42; Ben Ezra
  Synagogue (Maimonides
  Synagogue), 138, *139*, 140;
  Geniza, *140–1*; Karaite
  Synagogue, *140*, *141–2*
Calatayud, 57, 59
Calcutta, 153–4; Magen David
  Synagogue, *152–3*, 153–4
candelabrum (7-branched:

menora), 21, 22, 24, 27, 28, *28*,
  32, *34*, 88, *89*, 177, 181, *195*, 200;
  6-branched (Holocaust
  memorial), *195*
Capernaum synagogue (Kfar
  Nahum), 11, 18, *20*, 21, 25
Caribbean synagogues, 117, 122,
  124–7
Carpentras Synagogue, 113, *114*;
  Chair of Elijah, 113, *114*
Carvalho, S.N., *128*
Casale Monferrato synagogue, 90,
  92
'Casale Pilgrim', *141*, *145*
Castelo de Vide synagogue, *70–1*
Cavaillon Synagogue, *112*, 113–14,
  115
Chagall, Marc, 200–1
Charleston, Beth Elohim
  Synagogue, 127, *128*, 182, 184
Chicago, Anse Maariv
  Congregation, 184
China, Kaifeng Synagogue,
  158–63
Chodorow Synagogue, *109*, *111*
choirs, 170, 181, 182, 184
Cincinnati, B'nai Jeshurun, Plum
  Street Temple of Congregation,
  182, 184
Cleveland, Park Synagogue, *190*,
  191
Cochin Jews/synagogues, 149,
  154–8; caste system, 154;
  Paradesi Synagogue, 154, *155*,
  154–7, 158; Simhat Torah
  procession, 158, *158*
Cohen, Israel, 180–1
Cologne, Roonstrasse Synagogue,
  178; Synagogue, 37
Conegliano Veneto synagogue, *91*
consistorial synagogues, 167, *181*
Copenhagen Synagogue, *188*
Cordova, Church of Corpus
  Christi, 57, 68, *68–9*; Synagogue,
  58, 63, *63–4*, 113
Corinth, 11, 27, 28
courtyards, 18, 29, 34, 53, 54, 58,
  73, 98, *100*, 120, 134, 138, 142,
  144, *159*
Cracow synagogues, 93–6; Hoyche
  ('High') Synagogue, 94; Isaac
  Jacobowicz Synagogue, 94, 96,
  96–7; Old (Stara) Synagogue,
  93–4, *93–4*; Rema Synagogue,

94, 94–5, 96; Yom Kippur service, 97
Crystal Night (*Kristallnacht*) 41, 58, *166*, 185, *186*, 187
Curaçao, 124, 126–7; Mikve Israel Synagogue, *124, 126, 126*

Damascus, 11, 142
Dangoor, Rabbi Ezra Reuven, 142
Danzig, Great Synagogue, *186*
David, David and Lazarus, 127
Day of Atonement, 11, 53, 97, *121*, 143, 151, 158, *165*
Detroit, Beth-El Synagogue, 184
Divekar, Samuel Ezekiel, 149
Djerba, 138; el-Ghariba Synagogue, *134*, *135*, 138
Domenge, Jean, *159*
Dortmund, synagogues in, 185
Dresden Synagogue, 174
Dubrovnik Synagogue, *76–7*
Dura-Europos synagogue, 29, *31*, *32*

East Berlin synagogues, 188–9 *see also* Berlin
Eisenstat, Sidney, *195*
Elkins Park, Pennsylvania, Beth Shalom Congregation Synagogue, *191*, *191–2*, 195
El Paso, Texas, Mount Sinai Temple, *195*
En-Gedi, mosaic floor from synagogue at, *24*
En Neshut synagogue, *26–7*
Ernakulam synagogues, Cochin, 154–5
Eshtemoa synagogue, Judea, 19
Essen Synagogue, 180, *180*
Ethiopian Jews, 163–5
Eugenius IV, Pope (papal bull of 1434), 75
excommunication, 53, 94, 114, 117
Ezekiel, Prophet, 9; 'Vision of the Dry Bones', 13

Falashas *see* Beta Israel
Ferrara synagogue, 74
Fez, Danan Synagogue, *136*
Florence, Tiempo Israelitico Synagogue, 174, *174–5*
fortress synagogues, 100–5
four-pillar synagogues, 97, 99, 100, *101*, 110
Frankfurt synagogues, 50, 53, 168, *168*
funeral services, 53, 73
Fürth synagogue, 50, 51, *54–5*

Gajna synagogue, Ethiopia, *164*
Galilean synagogues, 17–19, 25, 138, 144, 180

Gamla synagogue, Golan Heights, 15–16, *16*
Gandhi, Mrs Indira, 154
Gaza, synagogue mosaic at, 21, *22*
geniza (depository), 13, 140–1, 144
Georgia (Russia), synagogues in, 189, 190
Gerona, Isaac el Cec Synagogue, 69
el-Ghariba Synagogue, Djerba, *134*, *135*, 138; Lag ba-Omer pilgrimage to, 135
ghettos, Jewish, 80–92, 187
Golan Heights, synagogues in, 15–16, *16*, 25, *26–7*
Goodman, Percival, 195
Gothic synagogues, 37, 46, 49, 59, 94, *94*; neo-, 174, 177, *183*, 184
Gottlieb, Maurycy, 97
Greek synagogues, 27
Grojec wooden synagogue, *109*
Gucci, Matteo, 94

Hadassah Synagogue, Jerusalem, Chagall's stained-glass windows, 200–1
al-Hakim, Caliph, 131
Hallel prayer, 58
Hammam-Lif Synagogue, 33, *34*, 34
Hammath-Tiberias, mosaic floor of synagogue at, 23
Hanover Synagogue, 177, *186*
hanukka lamp, 53
Harrison, Peter, 127, *129*
Hasid, Judah, 146
Hasidei Ashkenaz, 37
Hasidism, 110, *110*
hazzan (prayer leader), 38, *150*
Hebrew University, Israel: Hecht Synagogue, Mount Scopus campus, *202*; Israel Goldstein Synagogue, Givat Ram campus, *198*
Hebron, 145; Abraham Avinu Synagogue, *145*
Hecker, Zvi, *197*
Herod, King, 9, 12, *12*, 13, *15*
Herodion, 12, 13–14, *14–15*, 15
Herzl, Theodor, 174
Hettich, Jos. I., 47
Heu, Abraham, 43
Hitler, Adolf, 185
Holocaust memorials, 195
Hooghe, Romeyn de, *116*
hospices/hostels, 12, *12*, 21, 53, 58
Howland, Benjamin, *129*

Iconium, 11
Innocent IV, Pope, 58
Iraqi Jews/synagogues, 143; in India, *148*, 149, 153–4
Israel Institute of Technology Synagogue, Haifa, *199*

Isserles, Moses, 94, *94*, 97
Istanbul synagogues, 131–2
Izmir, Bikkur Holim Synagogue, *132*; Hevra Synagogue, *132*

Jacobson, Isaac, 169
Jerusalem, 11–12, *12*, 144–6, 196, 200; Belz Synagogue, 200; Great Synagogue, *200–1*; Hadassah Synagogue, 200–1; Hurva (or Judah Hasid) Synagogue, 146, *147*; Istanbul Synagogue, 145; Italian Synagogue, *91*; Johanan ben Zakkai Synagogue, 145, *146*, 200; 'Middle' Synagogue, 145; Prophet Elijah Synagogue, 145; Ramban Synagogue, 144–5, *145*; Theodotus inscription, 12, *12*; Tiferet Israel (or Nissim Beck) Synagogue, *130*, 146; Yeshurun Synagogue, *196*, *196*
Jerusalem-by-the-Riverside Synagogue, Surinam, 124
'Jerusalem Mishneh Torah', 72, 74
Jewish Religious Union, 151
'Joden-Savanne' settlement, Surinam, 124, *124*
Josephus, 9, 28
Judah ben Gedaliah, Rabbi, 71
Jurburg wooden synagogue, *107*

Kahn, Albert, 184
Kahn, Louis I, 191
Kaifeng Synagogue, China, 158, *159–62*, *162–3*
Kaliningrad Synagogue, *179*
Kaplan, Mordecai M., 190
Karaite Jews, 131, 141–2, 144
Karaite Synagogue, Cairo, *140*, 141–2
Kassel Synagogue, 176, *177*
Katzrin Synagogue, Israel, 26
Kennedy Airport, New York, International Synagogue, *193*
Kirchheim wooden synagogue, *110*
Kirchner, P.C., 52, *54*
Kitchener, Herbert (of Khartoum), 18

Lag ba-Omer pilgrimage to el-Ghariba Synagogue, 135
Lancut Great Synagogue, *105*
Leghorn, 74; Synagogue, 92, 187
Leipzig Mahzor, 38
Leipzig Synagogue, 174
Levantines, 74; Synagogue of the (Venice), 86, *86*
Libyan synagogues, 138
Lisbon, Great Synagogue, 71
Lisnitski, Israel ben Mordecai, *111*
Lloyd Wright, Frank, 191, *192*, 195
Loew, Rabbi Judah, 50

London, 122, 187; Bevis Marks Synagogue, 122, *123*, 187; Creechurch Lane Synagogue, 122; Great Synagogue, Duke's Place, 122, *123*; Petersburg Place, Bayswater, *177*; wartime bombardment of, 187
Longhena, Baldassare, *84*, 85
Lunéville Synagogue, *115*
Luria, Isaac, 146
Lutsk, fortress synagogue, *101–2*, 104
Lwow, Isaac Nachmanowicz (or Taz) Synagogue, 96

mahzor (festival prayer-book), 40, 78
Maimonides, Moses, 140
Mantua Synagogue, 75
Maon Synagogue, near Nirim, mosaic floor, 21, *221*
Masada, 8, *12–13*, *13*, *14*, 15
matzot oven/bakery, 34, *113*
Medzibezh, Podolia, *beth midrash* of Israel Baal Shem Tov, *110*
Mendelsohn, Erich, *190*, *191*
menora see candelabrum
mikveh see ritual bath
Miletus, synagogue in, 27
military synagogues, Israeli, *197*, *198*, 200
minyanim (prayer quorums), 187, 195
Mitzpeh Ramon military synagogue, *197*
Mocatta, David, 180
Mohiler Synagogue, *109*
Montefiore, Sir Moses, 180
Montreal, Shearith Israel Synagogue, 127, *128*
Moorish-style synagogues, 59–68, 135, 174, 184
mosaics, 21, *21–4*, 25, 27, 28, 32, *34*, *34*, 37, 66, 180, 195
moshavot synagogues, Israel, 196
Munich Synagogue, 169, 185
al-Mutawakkil, Caliph, 131

Nahmanides (or Ramban), 144, *145*
Napoleon I Bonaparte, 167, 172
Nazi destruction of synagogues, 41, 58, *166*, 185, *186*, 187
neo-Classical synagogues, 167, 172, *173*, 174, *177*, 184
neo-Gothic synagogues, 174, 177, *183*, 184
Newport, Rhode Island, Touro Synagogue, 127, *129*
New Year (*Rosh Hashana*), 52, *53*, *150*, 158
New York, Anshe Chesed Synagogue, 184, 195; B'nai

Jeshurun, Elm Street, 182, *182*; Central Synagogue, 184; International Synagogue, Kennedy Airport, *193*; Shearith Israel Synagogue, Central Park West, 127, 184; Shearith Israel Synagogue, Mill Street, 127, *127*, *182*; Temple Emanu-El (b.1868), 184; Temple Emanu-El (b.1929), *183*, 184
North Shore, Glencoe, Illinois, Congregation Israel, *194*
Nuremberg synagogues, Nazi demolition of (1938), 185; women's synagogue, 39

Obadiah of Bertinoro, 73, 142, 144
Oppler, Edwin, 176–7, 180
organs, 169, 170, 182, 184
Orléans synagogue, 27
Ostia, synagogue at, 32, *32*, 34

Padua synagogue, *90*
Palermo synagogue, 73
Paramaribo, Surinam, Neveh Shalom Synagogue, 124, *125*; Zedek va-Shalom Synagogue, 124, *125*
Paris, 167; Art Nouveau Synagogue, rue Pavée, 180; New Consistorial Synagogue, *181*; rue de la Victoire Synagogue, 180–1; Temple of rue Notre-Dame-de-Nazareth, 167, *181*
Passover, *53*, *56*, 138
Paul, St, 11
Paul IV, Pope (bull of 1555), 80
Pedro the Cruel of Castile, King, 66
Pentateuch, 9, 138
Pepys, Samuel, 122
Pesaro, 75; Spanish Synagogue, 79
Pfefferkorn, Johannes, 39
Philadelphia, Beth Israel Synagogue, 184; Knesseth Israel Synagogue, 184; Mikveh Israel Synagogue (c.1745), 127; Mikveh Israel Synagogue (1825), 184; (1963), *191*
phylacteries (*tefillin*), 144, 182
Picart, Bernard, *120*, *121*
Portuguese synagogues/Jewry, 68, *69–71*, 74
Potsdam Synagogue, 180, 185
Prague, *189*; Altneuschul, 46, *46–9*, 50, *94*, 177, 189; Maisel Synagogue, 177; New Year Service in, *52*; Pinkas Synagogue, 50
prayer-books, *36*, 40, 78
prayer leader (*hazzan*), 38, *150*
prayer room *see* shtiebel
prayer-shawls, *74*, 75, 144

Priene Synagogue, 27, *28*
Provençal synagogues, *112*, *113–14*, *114–15*
Pugin, A.C., *123*
pulpit or lectern, 170, 181
Purim, *53*

Ramat Aviv, Tel Aviv, *194*
Ramleh Synagogue, 144
ram's horn *see shofar*
Rawlins, I.J., *66*
reader's desk and platform (*bima*), 36, 38, 39, 41, 47, 49, 51, 52, 56, 58, 59, 62, 63, 66, 73, 74, 75, 78–9, 81, 85, 86, 89, 90, 92, *92*, 94, 96–7, 99, 104, *105*, 108, 113, 114, 115, 120, 122, 132, *133*, 137, 141, 142, 144, 146, 155, 169–70, 176, 181, 182, 184, 200, 201
Reform Jewry, 169–70, 172, 174, 181–2, 184, *194*
Regensburg Synagogue, 37, 46, *46*
Rejoicing of the Law, Feast of the (Simhat Torah), 50, 122, *133*, 138, 158, 190
Rhineland synagogues, 27, 37–50
ritual bath/washing, 15, *15*, 28, 30, 41, 42, 53, 113, 134
Roman Empire, 10–11, *12–13*, 17, 18, 21, 29
Romanesque synagogues, 37, 39, 174, 176–7, *177–9*, 183
Romano, Paolo, 96
Rome, 11, 27–8, 75, 80, 86, 88, *88–9*, 92; Castilian Synagogue, 88; Catalan-Aragonese Synagogue, 88, *89*; Central Synagogue, 92; ghetto synagogues, 86, 88, *88–9*, 92; New Synagogue, 88; Piazza delle Scole (Square of the Five Synagogues), *89*, 92; Sicilian Synagogue, 88; Temple Synagogue, 88, *88*, 92
Rosengarten, Albert, 180
Rowlandson, Thomas *123*
Rotterdam synagogues, 187
Rszesow fortress synagogue, 104

Safed, 145, 146; Ashkenazi 'Ari' Synagogue, *110*, 146, *147*; Isaac Aboab Synagogue, 146, *147*; Sephardi 'Ari' Synagogue, 146
St Louis, B'nai Amoonah Synagogue, *191*
Salonica, Great Talmud Torah Synagogue, *133*
Salzer, Erna, 42
Sanaa, Yemen, synagogues in, *143*, 143–4
San Francisco, Temple Emanu-El (1866), 184; (1926), 184

Sarajevo Haggada, *59*
Sardis Synagogue, 28–9, *29–31*
Sassoon, David, 144
Savannah, Georgia, Mikveh Israel Synagogue, 127
Schedia inscriptions, Egypt, 10
Schwartz, Samuel, 68
seating, seat ownership, 36–7, 59, 75, 132, 144, 169–70
Second World War, 187, 189, 190
seder (Passover eve home service), 53
Seesen Synagogue ('Temple of Jacob'), Germany, 169
Segal, Hayyim ben Isaac, 109
Segovia synagogues, 57, 62
Sermide Synagogue, ark from, *91*
Seville synagogues, 57
Shavuot, 53, 138
Shem Tov, Israel Baal, *110*
Shewata Synagogue, Ethiopia, *164–5*
Shiryon, Rabbi Kinneret, 194
shofar (ram's horn), sounding of, 17, 21, 22, 24, 32, 39, 52–3, 78, 120, 150, 177
shtiebls (prayer rooms), 110, 184
Shulhan Aruch (legal code), 46
siddur (prayer-book), 36
Siegen Synagogue, Nazi destruction of (1938), *186*
social hall/centre, 53, 55, 58, 191
Soviet Union, synagogues in, 188, *188–9*, 189–90, 202
Spain, synagogues, in, 27, 56–7, *57–68*, 69, 75
Speyer, synagogue at, 37, 39, 41, 50
Spinoza, Baruch, 124; excommunication of (1656), 114, 117
stained-glass windows, 37, 180, 195, 200–1
Stalin, Josef, 189
Star of David (*Magen David*), 177, 200
Stern, Henry A., 163
Stockholm, Great Synagogue, 170
Sullivan, Louis, 184
Surinam, 126; 'Joden-Savanne' settlement, *124*, 124; Paramaribo synagogues, 124, *125*
Susiya Synagogue, Judea, 19
Sussman, Eliezer ben Solomon, *110*
Sydney (Australia), Great Synagogue, *179*

Syrian synagogues, 27, 29, 142

Tabernacles, Feast of, 11, 17, 21, *53*, 138, 158, 163, 177
Tablets of the Law, 67, 68, 84–5, 89, 177, *177*, 200
Talmud, 11, 35, 37
Tashkent Synagogue, Uzbekistan, *188–9*
Tel Aviv, Diaspora Museum, 7; Great Synagogue, 196, *196*; Hechal Yehuda Synagogue, *199*
Temple, Jerusalem, 7, 10, 11, 32, 169, 177; destruction of first (6th century BC), 9; destruction of second (AD 70), 17; Women's Court, 25; *see also* Jerusalem temples, 169, 172; difference between synagogues and, 184
Tetuan, synagogue in *138–9*
Theodotus inscription, Jerusalem, *12*, 12
Tiberias Synagogue, 144, *145*
Toledo synagogues, 57; 'El Transito', 63, *65*, 66, 67, 68; Santa Maria La Blanca, 60–2, *62*, 68
Tomar Synagogue, 68, *69–70*
Torah, Torah scrolls, 10, 11, 13, 16, 21, 24, 25, 26–7, 28, *31*, 32, 38, 39, 52, 53, *53*, 57, 59, 62, 68, 72, 73, 75, *75*, 77, *105*, 132–3, *133*, 135, 138, 141, 149, 154, 158, *159*, 163, 195
Transjordan, 25, 144
Trapani Synagogue, 73
Tunis, Great Synagogue, *135*, 138
Turkey, synagogues in, 28, 131–2, *132*
twin-nave synagogues, 41, 46, *46*, 50, 93–4
Tykocin Synagogue, 105

Uriel da Costa, 124; excommunication of (1624), 114, 117
Uzbekistan synagogues, *188–9*, 189

Van der Laan, A., *120–1*
Veehuysen, I., *116*
Venice, 74, 80–6; Canon Synagogue, 81, 84; Great Ashkenazi Synagogue, *80–1*; 81, 82–3; Italian Synagogue, 86, *87*, 89; New Ghetto Square, *80–1*;

Spanish Synagogue, 81, *84–5*, 85–6; Synagogue of the Levantines, 86, *86*
Vienna, 177; Seitenstettengasse Synagogue, *172*, 172
Vilna, 100; Great Synagogue, 97, *99*; Old Klaus Synagogue, 97; Shulhof synagogue courtyard, *98*, *100*; Strashhun Library, *98*, *100*
Vilna Gaon, *100*

Walaka Synagogue, Ethiopia, *165*
Warsaw, Great Synagogue, Tlomacka Street, *173*
Washington, George, 127, *129*
wedding ceremonies, 53, *54*, *152*
White, Bishop William, 158
windows of synagogues, 18, 35–6, 62, 67, 68, 117; stained-glass, 37, 180, 195, 200–1
Wise, Isaac M., 184
Wizuny (Lithuania) wooden synagogue, *107*
Woerlitz Synagogue, 172
Wojnarski, Jan, *94*
Wolpa wooden synagogue, *106*
women rabbis/functionaries, 39, 194, 195
Women's Court, the Temple, 25
women's sections/galleries, 16, 25, 29, 38–9, 39, 41, 42, 50, *51*, *52*, 59, 63, 66, 75, 81, 86, 92, *103*, *106*, 108, 113, *114*, *119*, 122, 127, 134–5, 146, 155, 168, *168*, 170, *171*, *176*, 182, 191, 200
wooden synagogues, *51*, 103, 106–10
Worms Synagogue, 37, 41, 42–3, 46, 50, 93–4; post-war reconstruction of, 41, 188; Rashi Chapel, 41, *44–5*
Wurbs, drawing of Altneuschul by, *47*

Yamasaki, Minoru, 194
Yemen, 27, 134–5, 143, *143–4*
Yevsektzia Jews, Soviet Union, 189

Zabludow wooden synagogue, *103*, 108
Zealots, 12, *13*, 13–14, *15*
Zebulun tribe, 135
Zelwa synagogue, *108*
Zolkiew fortress synagogue, *104*